Finishing
Techniques for
Crochet

Finishing Techniques for Crochet

Pauline Turner

COLLINS & BROWN

First published in the United Kingdom in 2009 by
Collins & Brown
10 Southcombe Street
London
W14 0RA

An imprint of Anova Books Company Ltd

Photography by Michael Wicks (step-by-step)
and Becky Maynes (beauty)

ISBN 978-1-84340-473-6

A CIP catalogue for this book is available from the
British Library.

10 9 8 7 6 5 4 3 2 1

Reproduction by Rival Colour Ltd, UK
Printed and bound by SNP Leefung, China

This book can be ordered direct from the publisher.
Contact the marketing department, but try your
bookshop first.

www.anovabooks.com

Introduction

My mother taught me many craft and household skills but she never taught me to crochet. For that I have to thank her, as it meant I had to teach myself. Therefore, most of my life I have worked with my hands and can produce numerous things in a number of crafts.

As a full-time college lecturer I taught a mixture of craft skills for both vocational and non-vocational students for 15 years. It was after I had been teaching full-time for one year at my last college that my Head of Department informed me I was to teach crochet in the Autumn.

Not knowing crochet allowed me to explore, experiment and play with the crochet hook in many ways. I had such fun with the variety of hooks and materials available, the myriad colours and textures of yarns and the endless possible stitch combinations available.

The 'teacher' in me needed to understand how this fascinating world of crochet worked and so I analysed my processes. I discovered there is no right or wrong way to crochet, simply good ways and not so good ways. Often crochet playtime comes up with fabulous designs almost by accident. Most importantly the push to learn how to crochet enabled me to find the best ways of producing crochet efficiently.

Within the pages of this book there are lots of ideas to help you create crochet using techniques and tips that produce finished articles with professional-looking results. I sincerely hope you have as much enjoyment in trying out these ideas as I have had in writing about them and in the crocheting of them.

Getting Started

Strong foundations are the making of all good projects. Take time to understand the basic skills and equipment you will be using. With such a variety of supplies available, the choices you make will influence the end product you create.

1

Tools and Equipment

The equipment needed for crochet can be kept to a minimum. As with every craft, you can collect endless pieces and experiment with the latest gadgets – however, a few basic essentials are the key to a successful project.

Basic Requirements

You cannot crochet without a hook, some yarn or thread and a few other tools. The following list of basic equipment will help you to select the items that are the most appropriate for your project.

Hook Type

Hooks vary in shape and size. They can be made of metal, plastic or wood, with or without a handle. The key is to select a hook you will enjoy working with, which is suitable for the project. Whichever hook you choose, you need to check your tension when you start work – hooks of the same size from different manufacturers may give you slightly different results. Traditionally, hooks were classified as either thread hooks or yarn hooks.

Thread Hooks

Thread hooks are stiletto shaped, similar to the ones used for tambour embroidery, and are sometimes referred to as tambour or cotton hooks. These stainless-steel hooks come in sizes 0.60–2.50mm (US 1–14) and are used for fine-thread crochet. A thread hook that is larger than 1.6mm will probably look more like a yarn hook.

Yarn Hooks

Yarn hooks normally range from 2.50–16mm (US B–Q) although today you can purchase hooks that are even larger than the 16mm hook. A yarn hook is identified as such when the body or stem of the hook is even throughout, only narrowing as it merges into the hook head. Although yarn hooks are normally used with spun fibres, they are equally suitable for crocheting with craft materials. Some hooks are manufactured with a handle. (Sizes above 5mm do not need handles as the size of the shaft makes them quite comfortable to hold.) Handled hooks are ideal for anyone who finds it difficult to hold a narrow hook for any length of time, especially if she or he has stiff joints. The thickness of a handle makes it easier to grip; it is also warm to the touch, unlike metal. An alternative would be to purchase bamboo or wooden hooks.

Tunisian Crochet Hooks

There is another kind of crochet hook called a Tunisian crochet hook, which is as long as a knitting needle. Tunisian crochet is worked differently than ordinary crochet, looks different and requires very different finishing techniques on the whole.

Hook Size

The hook size is chosen to give the correct tension for the item being made. In garment-making, it needs to be one or two sizes larger than the knitting needle size recommended on the ball band, to allow for the extra strand of yarn lying within the structure of a crochet stitch. This applies to both yarn and thread. (But for an outdoor garment designed to withstand wind and water, you would need to go down a hook size to enable the stitches to sit tightly together.)

You may find that your tension varies each time you work on a piece – if you are tense, your stitches may be closer or smaller than the last time you worked on it. If that is the case, use a hook that is one size larger until you relax, then return to the original hook. The converse of this is that it is also possible for your stitches to be too loose when you resume your crochet: then you would need to go down a hook size. Remember, you are in control – your crochet hook is not!

Scissors

Sharp-pointed embroidery scissors are essential, but be careful that you do not accidentally snip any threads within the stitch structure. For cutting out templates or paper patterns, use scissors suitable for cutting paper. Should you decide to line a crocheted garment or bag, a pair of dressmaker's scissors will come in handy and can also be used for many tasks.

Safety Pins

Whenever you have to leave your work, place a safety pin in the last loop so the piece will not unravel. Safety pins are also useful for marking your work and for holding pieces of crochet together in readiness for joining (particularly so with the bulkier yarns). Coiless safety pins are best – with these the yarn cannot get stuck in the end.

Stitch Markers

Stitch markers may serve the same purpose as safety pins, but with continued use they sometimes break. Most stitch markers are lighter than metal safety pins and are therefore ideal for placing in the crochet as work progresses to mark decreases and increases.

Straight Pins

Long, straight pins with large heads are useful for pinning pieces of medium or lightweight crochet together. The head must be large enough to stay outside the work and not vanish inside the stitches.

Tape Measure and Ruler

A tape measure is of course essential for taking measurements. It can also be used to estimate your tension: when doing this it is vital to place the crochet on a smooth, flat surface. (If crochet is placed on top of a flat piece of fabric on a table, there is a chance that it will stick to the fabric and you will not measure the correct tension.)

I use a table and a ruler to work out my tension, and a tape measure for all other numerical information. With so many patterns available globally, I prefer a tape measure marked in both centimetres and inches.

Sewing Needles

Large-eyed tapestry or sewing needles are required for darning in the ends of the yarn, even though a crochet hook can be used for this purpose in some instances. Tapestry needles come in different sizes and have a blunt end instead of a sharp point, so that they do not split the yarn. Yarn needles can be purchased in either metal or plastic.

If you wish to attach beads as an embellishment, you will need a selection of beading needles. These are very fine with an extremely slender eye allowing the needle to pass through small beads. For adding a fabric lining to a pocket, bag or garment, ordinary sewing needles would be needed.

Buttons

Buttons are used both for decoration and as fasteners. If you wish, you can crochet buttons to match a garment. Use a button mould, an old button, a plastic ring or a bead as the base. Find out how to crochet buttons on page 82.

Zips

Zips that are closed at one end are suitable for purses, pockets or use as a decorative feature. For garments such as jackets, purchase heavier, open-ended zips.

Notebook

However good your memory is, over a period of time you will forget some of the methods, stitches, hooks, yarns and shaping you have used or have intended to use. Write down everything in a notebook, rather than on a scrap of paper – there's less chance of it getting lost.

Most importantly, when you are working on a design you will certainly get ideas on how you might like to finish the article or perhaps embellish it. The yarn and hook will begin to 'talk' to you and suggest ways of making the design even better. All of these ideas need to be recorded for possible future use. Not all ideas work: perhaps you will try one and be a little disappointed with the result – just occasionally the yarn or stitch does not blend in to make a truly creative and professional finish. But if that happens you can try another alternative. However proficient you are, it is only when you are actually working with the hook and yarn that your ideas are realised – and the results may not be what you expect.

Calculator

Despite being quite good at maths, I am afraid I would be concerned if I could not check my calculations with a calculator.

Divide the number of stitches between buttons and buttonholes evenly. I do not use a tape measure for calculating the space between stitches because when an equal number of stitches are used, the look of the article is balanced and pleasing to the eye. Of course it is essential that you have the same number of stitches for the button band as are on the buttonhole band!

Row Counter

Row counters are not used much in crochet but can come in handy. I use one if the pattern has a repeat of over eight rows. It is also useful when working with complex row and stitch changes.

Normally, crochet rows and stitches are easy to count, but if you are in any doubt use a row counter. Sometimes you may be unable to count the rows because of the texture incorporated into the crochet fabric. The alternative to a row counter is to use your notebook!

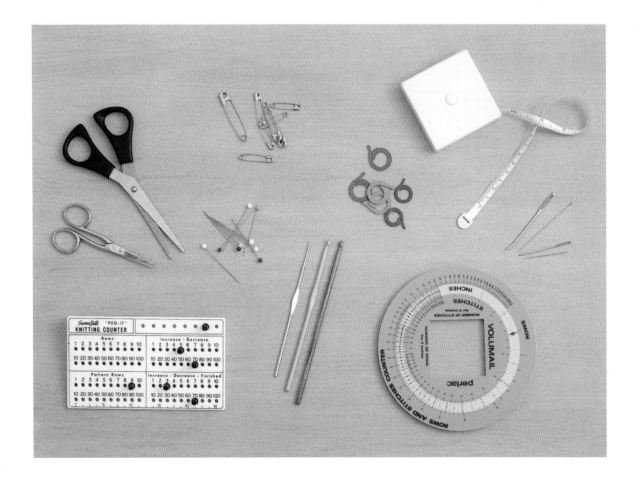

Yarns and Threads

One of the joys of crochet is that you can use many kinds of material: if it bends, you can crochet with it! Crochet is therefore very exciting to do. To produce original ideas that look professional, a high-quality finish is important. This means choosing the right yarn and selecting the correct hook size for what is being created.

People who do not spin, have never taken a textile course and who have only purchased yarn as recommended by the published pattern, may have a limited knowledge of the suitability of yarns for a particular project. Using a yarn that is unsuitable or simply not understanding the peculiarities of fibres and dyes can result in disappointment. The following very brief notes will help you to understand why your tension can seem to be erratic for no apparent reason.

Dye Colour

A dye can change both the weight and the thickness of a yarn. Some of the dyes incorporated into yarn have a physical weight and some are heavier than others. The result is that a specified weight in two different colours of the same yarn might yield differing meterages (yardages). The way the dye is absorbed will also sometimes create a difference in both the elasticity and thickness of the yarn.

Natural Fibres

Undyed yarns containing natural fibres vary in colour. This can be because of soil composition, moisture and sun (if of plant origin); or because of the amount of oil and pigmentation (if of animal origin). This affects the colour when dyed and is the reason why it is essential to purchase yarn from the same dye lot.

Acrylic or Manmade Fibres

Acrylic or manmade fibres spun for garment-making are often stretchy. So if the fingers you use to control the yarn as you work grip it too tightly, the yarn will become thinner. Once released, it will go back to its natural state, shortening the stitches and often producing tighter stitches.

Twists

The more twists per centimetre within a yarn, the harder-wearing and longer-lasting it will be, making it very suitable for accessories and garments that are worn frequently. This kind of yarn does not fluff up or pill. Yarns with very few twists, such as Icelandic yarns, are prone to accumulate fluffy balls of yarn on the outside of the garment. If you work the yarn from the outside of the ball as you crochet, it often puts a twist into the yarn. Using a textured stitch such as post stitch also reduces pilling.

Space Dyed Yarn

Space dyed yarn creates different challenges. Long, even stretches of colour tend to make colour blocks. Irregular long stretches of colour produce a Fair Isle or jacquard effect, rather than thin lines of colour. Space dyed yarns with short stretches of colour have a quite different outcome. Remember that crochet uses more yarn per centimetre than knitting, so a variegated yarn that looks good in a knitted piece will change colour more frequently in crochet. This can produce a fabric that is almost too busy.

Shiny Yarns

Shiny yarns such as rayon, Lurex and others containing viscose fibres, have a habit of twisting and unravelling from the ball or cone as you crochet. To prevent this, place the yarn in a plastic bag with a rubber band around the opening, close to the yarn but with just enough room for the yarn to flow. This helps to keep the ball intact.

Slub and Nubby

For slub and nubby textured yarns, use a hook size suitable for the thickness of the slub or nub. Do not select a hook size suitable for the thinner yarn lying between the nubs. If you choose the smaller hook, you will be very disappointed.

Mohair, Angora and Other Natural Hair

These fibres need to breathe. Use a much larger hook than the size of knitting needle recommended on the yarn wrapper – go up three to four sizes for the first trial piece of crochet needed to calculate the tension. The hairs in mohair yarn should not need to be brushed once the yarn has been crocheted.

Chenille, Silk and Lurex Threads

Chenille, some silks, some Lurex threads and some softly twisted yarns may not wear very well. These kinds of yarn should only be placed where they will experience little wear and tear. Avoid placing them in the back of a garment where it can rub against chairs or on the inside of collars – the rest of the collar should be fine. In addition, avoid using above pockets, elbows and cuffs; also for skirts.

Mercerised Cotton

This thread has undergone an extra finishing process, which protects the cotton from fading caused by light, laundering or atmospheric dust.

If, when following a pattern, you change the specified yarn to one you prefer, work a swatch to make sure that the tension is the same, using the hook recommended in the pattern.

Preparation and Calculation Skills

Accurate measuring is essential for a wonderfully finished garment which delights you and the person for whom it is made. Check that you have all the measurements and then make your decision as to how much ease the garment needs for comfort and suitability of the design.

Changing a Size or Measurement Given in a Pattern

Patterns are produced according to a standard set of body measurements. However, very few people are a standard size. If you want an accurate fit, you need to compare your measurements with the body size measurements given for the pattern. Use the table on page 17 for this purpose. Measure all the relevant points shown on the sketch on page 17.

Some patterns indicate where you can shorten or lengthen the body, sleeve or even a pocket. Most do not. The following notes should help you change a pattern to the size required without it looking ugly.

Lengthening or Shortening Body Length

Look for a part of the upper body pattern where there is no decreasing for the armhole or neck and where increasing for any waist shaping has been completed. Add or reduce the number of rows within the area of straight rows.

Lengthening or Shortening a Sleeve

There are two areas on a sleeve where it should be possible to lengthen or shorten it. From the elbow to the wrist there are usually a number of rows that do not contain increasing (if worked from the cuff) or decreasing (if worked from the armhole down). This is the best place to add or reduce the number of rows.

However, in some sleeve patterns there will be an area at the top of the sleeve just below the sleeve cap where straight rows might be included (that is, before increasing begins if working downward to the cuff or decreasing stops if working up from the cuff). This could be an alternative place to lengthen or shorten the sleeve, depending upon stitch design and the shape of the sleeve itself.

Lengthening or Shortening a Design Below the Waist

Unless the design is a loose-fitting longline jacket, any lengthening or shortening below the waist needs to take into consideration some kind of shaping. To lengthen or shorten a skirt or coat, it would require two rows to be added evenly between the increase rows for added length and for two rows to be removed between the increase rows to shorten it. Shortening a skirt, dress or shaped coat pattern is more of a challenge than making it longer.

NOTE: During the making of a full-length garment, it is necessary to pin the waist edge of the garment to a padded hanger for at least 48 hours and leave it to hang. This lets the stitches settle as gravity takes over and at the same time allows any crinkles in the fibre to straighten out.

Changing the Position of the Hip

Standard body measurements place the widest part of the lower body at the hips, 20–25cm (8–10in) below the waist. But not everyone has the widest part of their lower body at the hips – for me it is only 10cm (4in) below the waist and therefore I need to adjust the fullness of patterns to avoid looking like the famous 'tyre baby'.

To accommodate a wider girth of this nature, work the increases as quickly as the pattern will allow, adding additional rows below the increases to replace those not worked earlier.

Even when the widest girth is at a lower point than 10cm (4in) below the waist, I would not suggest that you lengthen any increases incorporated for the hip measure from the waist. The higher increases in the fabric will give a flattering swing as the garment is worn.

Male Measurements

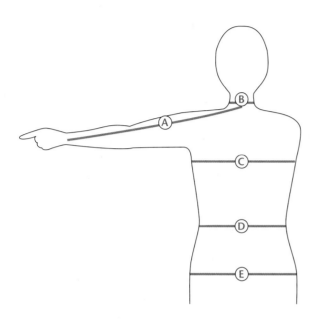

Female Measurements

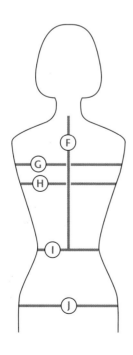

Measurements Table

	Standard size	Your Measurement	Ease allowance	Depth of border
Bust/chest (G & H)				
Waist (D & I)				
Hip (E & J)				
Back width (C)				
Length from nape of neck to waist (F)				
Length from nape of neck to hip				
Length from nape to base of design				
Back neck size (B)				
Shoulder width				
Depth of armhole				
Depth of head and neck (for hood)				
Sleeve length with cuff (A)				
Wrist circumference				
Pocket width				
Pocket depth				

Widening or Narrowing the Neck

Can I suggest that you do not adjust the shape of the neck opening on the body of a jumper unless the neck is really tight? Instead, use the border or collar to make the neck wider or narrower.

To widen the neck, do the following. As you work the first row or round directly onto the garment's neck edge, instead of placing one stitch per stitch or row end along the neck opening, use the front loop of one stitch and the back loop of the same stitch to create more stitches – thus widening the neck. The increases are not noticeable and the additional stitches will give the neck stretch. Space any increases evenly around the neck after having worked out how many stitches you require.

To make the neck tighter, decrease evenly around the neck opening by working two stitches together.

Changing the Size of the Armhole

A woman with very thin arms will feel uncomfortable if the armhole on a sleeveless top is too deep. So on a garment without sleeves, merely start the armhole shaping later and reduce the number of rows to the shoulder. If the armhole on a garment with sleeves is made smaller, be sure to adjust the sleeve pattern to match the new opening, making the upper part of the sleeve narrower to correspond.

Conversely, some people have quite muscular upper arms and a small armhole would be very uncomfortable when bending and stretching. In this instance, reduce the number of rows to the armhole and start the shaping of the armhole sooner to allow it to become deeper and add extra rows from the shaping to the shoulder. If the garment has sleeves, please remember to adjust the sleeve pattern, increasing or decresing the width at the top of the sleeve or in the sleeve cap to match the new armhole depth.

Calculating Ease

Most styles of garment worked in yarn include an ease allowance for comfort when the body moves. The amount of ease required is determined by the yarn chosen to achieve the garment's shape and to suit its use. On average, the ease allowance is 10cm (4in). When using tightly twisted yarn that is not very elastic or flexible, it may be necessary to increase the allowance to 15cm (6in). Yarns with almost no twist may require more than the standard 10cm (4in) of ease. On the other hand, where a yarn is soft either because it has fewer twists per inch or because the fibres tend to stretch, an ease allowance of 5cm (2in) should be sufficient.

Loose Longline Jackets

When the style of the garment goes down to the hips and has no shaping included, the hip measure would be a suitable measure for the bust. This can result in too much ease allowance being made for the bust. In a man's jumper, you may still need to include ease because a man normally has slimmer hips than a woman.

Batwing and Dolman Sleeves

When working batwing or dolman sleeves, you don't need to decide how much or how little ease to add. As the shape commences from below the bust for a dolman sleeve and extends from the waist with a batwing sleeve, there is no demarcation line for the armhole and the fullness of the sleeve allows ease of movement, eliminating the need to include ease in the bust and chest calculations.

Lacy Patterned Designs

Unlike most textiles, crochet does not always require ease. This applies to any loose, open and lacy crochet fabrics. The chain and slip stitch net fabric used for string bags and vests is a perfect example of this. This fabric wants to mould to whatever shape it contains and so it is not necessary to allow for ease – it simply adjusts itself.

Beautiful crochet lace fabrics in fabulous patterns do look better without ease. The lack of ease allows the fabric to stretch over the body, which both flatters the figure and shows off the design to its best advantage. As long as there is sufficient openness in the lace design, it will sculpt to the body as it moves, in the same way as the string bag. If you were to add ease to a lace top in thread, the lace patterns would crumple together and the pattern might not be seen.

Measuring the Tension

There is no need to work a tension to 'suit the yarn'. Rather, have the tension suit the purpose of the article being made. Before beginning the actual crocheted project, a swatch should be worked and the tension measured. If you are following a pattern, it will inform you of the number of stitches and rows you should have using the hook, yarn and stitch pattern suggested for their test piece. Observe how the swatch feels and looks. You can then decide if the hook is the right size. Any hook size can be used, but this will depend upon the effect you want to achieve.

Always make a swatch large enough to take measurements accurately. I suggest you work a 13cm (5in) square for yarns that are sport weight or thinner. This allows the first and last stitches in the rows to be ignored as the end stitches may be tighter than the rest of the piece. It is not unusual for the first 2–4 rows to be worked at a different tension than the body of the work, and therefore it is advisable to avoid including those rows in your calculations. Yarn that is thicker than sport weight can require a swatch as big as 25cm (10in), but usually 18–20cm (7–8in) is sufficient. This will depend upon the stitch pattern recommended for checking your tension. A small variation in stitch size, when calculating the measure, can make a big difference to the finished piece.

On a Roll

I always recommend that prior to measuring the swatch, you roll it from side to side, then pull it gently to elongate the stitches. This process simulates the effect of gravity, which will affect the crochet stitches when the garment is worn.

◄ Lay the swatch on a smooth, flat surface. Please avoid using your knee or the arm of a chair to save time. Stroke the swatch gently from the bottom to the top before measuring, to simulate the way the fabric will stretch when worn. If this step is omitted, the article can end up too narrow and too long. Do not stroke the swatch sideways unless the pattern has been worked in vertical rows!

Calculating the Amount of Yarn or Thread

When trying to work out the amount of yarn or thread to use, the following steps are most useful.

How to Calculate the Amount of Yarn or Thread	1. Calculate the number of stitches and rows to 'x' centimetres (inches), remembering to stroke the crochet stitches lengthwise before measuring.
	2. Decide whether to allow, or not to allow, ease.
	3. Look at the design. Wherever possible, eliminate seams to reduce the design to the minimum number of separate pieces in order to avoid unnecessary joining, which not all crochet workers can do neatly.
	4. Have the pattern shapes, or the written pattern, ready before beginning to crochet. If you have chosen a different yarn to the one specified, calculate the amount you will need to complete the piece. Work a swatch in the appropriate stitch pattern, using the proper hook in the yarn that you plan on using. Stop at this point. Measure the area of the swatch (square cm/square in) and/or add up all the stitches. Then to figure out the amount of yarn you will need for the entire project, tear out the swatch and measure the amount of yarn used. Then calculate the number of stitches or area of the entire piece, divide by the number in/area of the swatch, then multiply by the length of yarn in the swatch. This will tell you how much you will need for the entire piece.

Alternatively, multiply the meterage (yardage) in a ball of the recommended yarn by the number of balls required ('x'). Then look at the meterage (yardage) on the ball band of the yarn you want to use ('y'). Divide 'x' by 'y'. Round up this amount to the next whole number to give the number of balls required. Make an allowance (just an estimate) for extra yarn for joining, making buttons, tags and other embellishments.

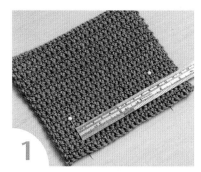

1 Lay the swatch out flat. Count the number of sts between the pins to give the number of sts per 10cm (4in).

2 Count the number or rows between the pins to give the number of rows per 10cm (4in).

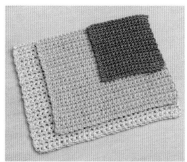

▲ Different hook sizes or different yarns to those recommended in the pattern change the size of the swatch.

Producing Perfect Crochet Fabrics

Once you have learned the basics,
you can move on to the skills and techniques
that will ensure you create a perfectly finished
project. With the valuable techniques and
know-how at your fingertips, you'll be able
to create your project of choice.

2

Technical Know-How

Finishings, fastenings and the execution and type of join chosen are all important for creating a perfect and professional finish. These include all the knots, chains used and edges employed throughout the project.

The Slip Knot

All crochet begins and ends with one loop on the hook. The loop on the hook made by a slip knot enables all other stitches to be worked. A slip knot is exactly that – a knot that slips to tighten the loop around the hook. The knot can slip from the short end of the yarn or it can slip from the ball end. A slip knot made from the short end of the yarn can be tightened in such a way that it disappears into the fabric being made. The slip knot that is tightened from the ball end leaves a blip or bump that remains visible.

▲ Making a slip knot from the short end of the yarn.

Knot Again

The only time a slip knot needs to be made from the ball end is when working a narrow braid or using an exceptionally slippery yarn – to prevent the knot from becoming loose.

▲ Slip knot made from the short end (left) and ball end (right).

Foundation Chains

The foundation chain is important as it gets the project off to a good start. You have to choose the right foundation chain for the project and select the best way to insert the hook before working any further on the pattern.

Normal Foundation Chain

The standard foundation chain requires the hook to catch the yarn in the hook head and pull it through, thus replacing the loop that was on the hook. Using a yarn hook (not one specifically manufactured for thread), the loop should fit snugly round the stem of the hook to create the correct tension. When you crochet into the chain to create your first row, have the smooth side of the chain facing (see bottom example, right).

▲ The wrong or rough side of the chain (top) and right or smooth side of the chain (bottom).

Double Foundation Chain

This produces a chain that is visible after it has been worked into for the body of the article. Each stitch is a double crochet with a built-in chain underneath it.

1
Ch2, insert hook in first ch, yo and pull through. Yo and pull through 2 loops on hook (forms the ch).

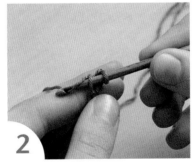

2
There is now one strand at the side of the ch. *Insert hook in LH side of the last ch, yo and pull through, yo and pull through 1 loop on hook (ch).

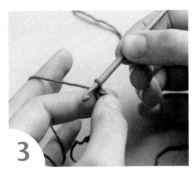

3
Yo and pull through both loops on the hook (dc). Rep from * until foundation ch is the length required.

Purl or Picot Foundation Chain

The purl or picot foundation chain is little remembered and infrequently used. It is ideal for projects worked in thread and provides the illusion of a picot edge. On dainty items, it saves adding a finishing border.

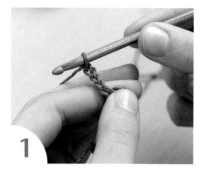

1

To begin, make a slip knot followed by 4 ch. Work one crochet into the first ch made. *Ch4.

2

Insert hook into the centre of the first of these four ch.

3

Work 1 dc.

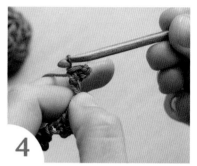

4

Repeat from * to length of foundation ch required.

Fastening Off

Fastening off in crochet is quite simple. Once the last stitch has been worked, make one chain. Cut the thread, leaving a length that is long enough to weave in the end.

1

Pull the cut end through the loop that was on the hook after making the chain.

2

Pull tight. It appears to have removed the chain and replaced it with a little knot very close to the last stitch. With a yarn or tapestry needle, weave in the end carefully, ensuring that it does not show on the right side of the fabric.

Working into the Foundation Chain

Counting the hoop of the chain stitch as two strands and the straight strand behind as one, the chain stitch is comprised of three strands of yarn. When inserting the hook to make the first row of stitches, you can choose to pick up two strands or just a single strand of yarn. With the smooth side of the chain facing, insert the hook so that one strand is below the hook and two strands are on top. The result is a neat 'buttonhole' finish similar to sewn buttonholes in material. Repeat this process to the end of the foundation chain.

If you pick up only a single strand of yarn, the result is a deeper edge, which is ideal when working with heavily twisted yarns that are not too thick or when working with threads. Unfortunately this method gives the edge a very ragged and untidy look if you are working with softly spun acrylics, mixed fibres or fashion yarns of irregular thicknesses.

Straight and Decorative Edges

There is no one right way to crochet, as each method has its own strengths and equally its own weaknesses. For fabrics that have to be seamed, it is better to have a very straight edge than an attractive picot or purl finish.

Producing Straight Edges

Work 1 ch at the end of the row to raise the hook to the level of the next dc row. Turn the work away from you rather than toward you. This leaves a smooth chain facing you when you come to the end of the row.

A Picot or Purl Edge

This is a twist on the standard straight edge, giving the garment a lovely decorative edge.

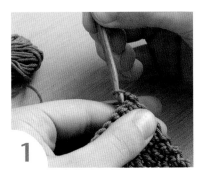

Do not work into the first st of the row (under the turning ch); place first st in the next st. This beginning ch will count as the first dc of the row.

At the end of the row, when it may look as if all the sts have been worked into, place one more st into the turning ch of the previous row.

▲ At the beginning of the row, work 2 ch. Work 1 dc in first st (at the base of 2 ch). At the end of the row, omit working into the turning ch.

Treble Crochet

Approximately half of all crocheters will only need to work a two chain turning chain when working a fabric of treble crochet. Patterns will state that you should turn your work with three chains, but unless you were taught to crochet in thread with very fine hooks, there is a strong possibility three chains will be taller than the size of the treble crochet worked. This is particularly true when crocheting with yarn that contains some elasticity. If the beginnings of the rows look untidy and loose, reduce the turning chains to two.

Double Trebles and Long Stitches

Should there be gaps at the beginning of rows with double trebles and other tall stitches, use the 'increase decrease' technique below to remove the gap.

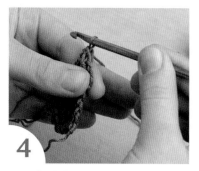

Work the necessary turning ch for the height of the st, begin the first st in the same place as the turning ch.

Work the first st until two loops are left on the hook.

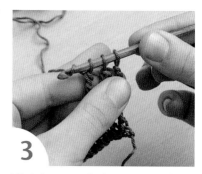

Work the next st in the next st until there are three loops left on the hook.

Yo and pull through all three loops. The post of an extra st has been placed in the gap but by working two st together, the number of sts remains the same.

▲ This is the standard way of working double trebles and shows clearly how gaps can appear at the side of the fabric.

▲ This is the way the fabric will look – without gaps – once the 'increase decrease' technique has been worked.

Increasing and Decreasing

A diagonal line is longer than a vertical line. Crochet uses turning chains to lift the hook to the level of the next row. When increasing in double crochet, one side is kept straight using only one chain to turn, but at the side where the work slopes, two chains are used to turn. This prevents distortion to the horizontal line of the stitch pattern.

Increasing

In crochet, there is nothing easier than increasing the number of stitches. Simply place two stitches where there would normally be only one. With most yarns and threads, you can insert the hook into the same hole in the same way as the first stitch. However, there are some yarns where it is advisable to use a different method. With heavily twisted or thick yarns, for example, an ugly and noticeable hole can result. This can be prevented by working the two stitches in different places within the same stitch.

▲ In this sample, increases have been worked the normal way on the right and the recommended way on the left.

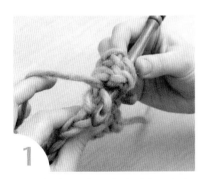

Work the first st into the back loop only.

Work the second st into the front loop only. In this way the two sts spread along the top of the st containing the increase, rather than forcing the st open and creating a hole.

Continue increasing in this way until the desired result is achieved.

Decreasing

It may seem easiest to skip a stitch for a decrease, but instead of creating a smooth slope, the result is a series of steps. Necks and armholes do not have steps – therefore avoid decreasing in this way unless it is a design feature.

To create a smooth line, work one stitch until two loops remain on the hook and the next stitch until three loops remain. Yo and pull the yarn through all three loops. This method of decreasing applies to all stitches except the half treble crochet.

▲ In this sample, decreases have been worked by skipping a stitch (on the left) and by tr2tog (on the right) – the recommended way.

Decreasing in Half Treble Crochet

1

At the beginning of a row, turn with only one ch instead of the usual two chs. Insert the hook in the same place as the turning ch without wrapping the yarn over the hook.

2

Yo, insert the hook into the next st.

3

Pull the yarn through to the front to give four loops on the hook. Yo and pull through all four loops. This gives the diagonal a backward slant.

4

At the end of a row, work to within the last 2 sts of row, then yo, insert the hook into the next to the last st, yo, insert the hook into the next st and pull the yarn through to the front.

5

Insert the hook into the last st without wrapping the yarn over first.

6

Yo and pull through all four loops.

7

Make one htr decrease at the end of the row.

The Rogue Stitch

Half treble crochet does not conform to the general principles of crochet: it has three strands of yarn at the top of the crochet stitch instead of two. For this reason, the half treble crochet sometimes requires separate technique information.

Raglan Shaping

The design line of raglan shaping in sleeves and at the armhole edge of the body does not show as clearly as it does in knitting. One way to accentuate the design line is to work into the back loop of the stitch before the decrease at the beginning of a row and after the decrease at the end of the row when the front of the work is facing. This leaves a small line on every alternate row where the front loop is left unworked. This 'marking' stitch can be left as it is or used to make a decorative finish – such as embroidery or surface crochet stitches – once the garment has been completed.

The principle of working a raglan shaping is to ensure that the first and last stitches remain constant. Depending on the thickness of the yarn, three or four stitches will be crocheted before working a decrease at the beginning of the row and the same number of stitches will be worked after the decreases at the end of the row.

▲ To accentuate the design line, tambour style surface crochet can be worked over the line created by the decrease.

Decreasing for Darts

Sometimes, with garments designed for a fuller figure or very fitted garments, it is necessary to include darts. The darts can be at the bust, neck, shoulders, waist or hips. Most of the darts will be vertical and therefore the normal increase or decrease methods already described are sufficient. However, sometimes it is necessary to incorporate a dart horizontally and that will require using a shortrowing technique.

In treble crochet, look at the distance from the side seam to the bust prominence. Divide this measurement into thirds. Crochet from the seam toward the bust prominence, for one third of the measure, in treble crochet. Work half of the next third in half treble crochet and the last part of the second third in double crochet. The next and last stitch for that row should be a slip stitch, which is not noticeable in the fabric. Turn the work and slip stitch over the double crochet, double crochet over the half treble crochet, half treble crochet for half of the treble crochet stitches of the previous row, finishing with treble crochet for the remainder of the row.

▲ This shows a dart worked in double crochet.

Joining in Yarn

Sometimes it seems wasteful to start a new ball of yarn at the end of a row, as the stitch height of many of the stitches used in the patterns is quite tall. When using luxury yarns and where a design has tall stitches incorporated in the garment, it would not be sensible to always join in a new ball at the end of a row. (Obviously it can be easier to join in a new ball of yarn at the end of row when there is very little yarn left to use.) Instead, join the yarn in the middle of a row: the methods I recommend are both secure and invisible.

Joining Yarns No Thicker Than Worsted

1

In a flat or textured piece of crochet or in some solid sections of an open or lacy design, crochet a st with the old yarn to the point where the hook has drawn the yarn through to the front.

2

Finish the st with the new yarn.

3

Lengthen the loop on the hook and make it temporarily secure.**

4

Weave the two ends of yarn through the back strand at the top of each st for 4–5 sts. Leave one end of yarn and continue for a further 2–3 sts with the one remaining strand. This creates a gradual tapering effect that is less obvious than stopping with both ends in the same st.

5

Return to the loop on the hook and crochet along the row in the usual way, inserting the hook in precisely the same way as you were doing prior to joining in the new yarn.

Joining Yarns Thicker Than Worsted

1 Work Steps 1–3 on page 33 to **. Take only one of the ends of yarn and loop through the back strand of the next 5–7 sts.

2 Return to the remaining end and weave that up the side of the st, where the new yarn was joined.

3 Turn the work and loop this second end through the front strands of the next few sts now facing.

4 By turning the work and weaving the second end through the front of the sts, the ends are hidden on the same side of the fabric.

Twist and Shout

Should you be working a yarn or thread that is tightly twisted, it is possible that placing two yarn ends in the same place may be noticeable. If that is the case, use the method described on the left.

Joining Yarns in Lacy and Open Designs

The method I use for any crochet where there is no obvious place to anchor the thread or yarn or in any style of crochet where there are long loops incorporated, is to sew the two yarns together to form one continuous thread.

Take a large-eyed sewing needle with a pointed end and thread the end of the new yarn through the old one. It is important you take the new thread at least 10–15cm (4–6in) into the old thread so that there is sufficient length in this double thread to make one full stitch of crochet or more.

Before crocheting with the continuous strand of yarn, gently tug both yarns so that the ends can disappear into what is now an unbroken thread.

Cut away ends that have not emerged into a single thread. Continue to crochet, being careful not to pull too hard on the thread containing the two ends.

Joining Lurex and Other Slippery Threads

Take a deep breath before you read this information! It does rather go against all we have ever been taught to do.

Incorporate the new yarn using one of the three methods already described. Before leaving the end, take an ordinary dressmaker's pin and dip the point into fabric glue. (Fabric glue usually has a latex base to provide flexibility and for washing purposes.) Carefully place this glue inside the stitch where the end of the yarn rests. Repeat for the end of the second yarn. Leave to set before continuing to crochet.

Creating a Professional Finish

Finishing techniques are one of the most important aspects of making a crocheted project. A perfect piece of crochet could prove unsuccessful if it is carelessly finished or the last stages are not given the same attention as the bodywork.

3

Pressing and Joining

Knowing how to produce invisible seams and recognising when you should or should not press your crocheted pieces are skills which will go a long way to producing perfect crocheted items.

Pressing Crochet

Because crochet is a fabric that automatically incorporates texture due to the way the stitches are constructed, pressing should be avoided wherever possible in order to retain texture. However, there are occasions when pressing is essential.

When to Press	1. Thread crochet is normally improved by pressing. Household items such as doilies and table centres worked in thread do require pressing (see Block Pressing, below)
	2. Some borders, corners, collar edgings or appliqué flowers worked in yarn might require a very light press. However it is important that the characteristics of the stitches and the design are not altered.
	3. Symmetrical motifs worked in a yarn that is not 100 per cent cotton or linen may need pressing. Motifs crocheted as part of a larger article might require pressing to ensure they are all the same size before being joined together. A word of warning – do not press anything until you have pressed the tension swatch to see what happens. Some fibres stretch with heat or water, while others may shrink. The motif can look very different after heat or steam has been applied!
	4. Avoid pressing any fabric incorporating surface crochet or raised stitches. The exception to this is when pressing thread crochet. However, clusters and puff stitches can flatten even in thread crochet, while post stitches and popcorns hold their texture.
	5. Many acrylic fibres will stretch if the pressing is done using a damp cloth.
	6. If absolutely necessary, background fabrics such as those made with double crochet, trebles or double trebles can be lightly pressed.
Basic Method of Pressing	1. Pin or smooth the crochet onto a flat surface, for example an ironing board. For a very large item, a folded blanket placed on a table is a useful substitute. I have even placed a blanket on the floor when an article will not even fit on a table.
	2. Use a clean white cotton cloth as a pressing cloth. Dampen it thoroughly. A man's handkerchief, a torn pillow case or part of a sheet are practical fabrics to use for this purpose.
	3. Place the cloth carefully over the crochet, taking care not to move the item being pressed.
	4. Press a hot iron, set at a temperature for cotton, in the centre of the cloth. Lift the iron and put it onto the cloth next to the place previously pressed. Do not drag the iron over the pressing cloth: simply press down and lift. Continue until the whole of the article has been pressed. Should you need to use the pressing cloth again, dampen it thoroughly once more.
	5. When the whole area has been pressed, remove the cloth taking care not to disturb the crochet.
	6. If at all possible, do not move the crochet until the moisture from the pressing cloth has evaporated.
Block Pressing	Block pressing is a way to ensure that a motif or larger article is pressed evenly. See page 39 for instructions on how to do it.
	Once the pressing is complete, put the item out of harm's way to completely dry out. Children, pets and open windows in a dusty area are the biggest danger to crochet at this stage. Once the article is in a safe place, remove the pins. I often cover the crochet (still pinned to a blanket) with another white cloth and pop it either under the bed or beneath a mat lying on a carpet.

Block Pressing

◀ First, pin the work to a blanket with pins, starting from the centre of each side. For squares, circles, hexagons and octagons, follow the order given in the photo when positioning the pins. It is tempting to start with one pin and then work in a clockwise or anticlockwise direction, but please do not, as it usually results in a mis-shaped motif or article.

Joining the Work

One of the giveaways that can determine whether or not an item looks 'homemade' or professionally fashioned is the way in which sections are joined. Choose the method of joining that is the most suitable for the article being made. Always take time to make sure the rows and the stitches of the crochet are matched perfectly.

Double Crochet Join

A join made with double crochet allows the work to 'give' during wear. It is a neat join when worked on the wrong side of the fabric and is particularly useful for garments that require the seams to move with the design.

1

2

Pin the two pieces of crochet together with right sides facing. Through the top of the sts on both pieces, work a dc picking up two strands of yarn on each piece – four strands in all.

Work a dc for each st, using the same yarn and the same hook as for the two pieces of crochet being joined.

Smooth Operator

With a crisp, smooth yarn, experiment with three ways of making the double crochet join to see which you like best.
1. Pick up the front loop on the piece nearest and the back loop on the second piece.
2. Pick up the back loop first, then the front loop.
3. Use a crab stitch join (page 41).

◀ Once completed, the double crochet join is almost invisible.

Slip Stitch Join

Slip stitch is a firm stitch and does not 'give' during wear. It is ideal for joining pieces in items such as purses, bags, slippers and other articles that need to have the pieces of crochet stay in place. When a slip stitch join is used on a garment such as a jacket, skirt or long jumper, there is a possibility that some of the softer yarns will relax a little during wear. Should this happen, the slip stitches will stay in place and the seams will be distorted. So while the fabric is being made, it is important to take precautions to prevent the crochet from relaxing.

Crab Stitch Join

Seams can be decorative. With wrong sides together, pin the two pieces of crochet together. Work crab stitch on the right side, using the same yarn or thread as the body of the work to create a strong design line. For a very noticeable join, crochet the two pieces together with a row of double crochet, returning with a row of crab stitch.

Insert hook under two strands on both pieces of crochet.

Check that there are two loops on the hook.

Complete the crab st (see page 57 for instructions).

◄ The result is three-dimensional, therefore this method should only be selected when this type of join is part of the overall design. For even more emphasis, the joining rows can be worked in a contrast colour.

Faggot Join

Open and lacy crochet fabrics need to keep the look of the design, even in the joining. Seaming pieces together using a faggot-style join is an excellent answer. A faggot join spreads the seam and therefore the pieces that are being connected will need to be slightly smaller than those being joined with double crochet or crab stitch.

1 Join in the yarn at the end of one of the pieces. Ch 3.

2 Sl st in the end st of the second piece of crochet. Ch 3.

3 Skip one st on the first piece, sl st into the next st space. Ch 3. Skip one st on the second piece, sl st into the next st space. Repeat steps until the seam is completed.

▲ It may be necessary to chain 2 to give a straight edge or work longer chains to match the laciness of the motifs.

Design Time

The faggot join – using just one chain instead of three – can be used as a design feature, producing a decorative join in solid fabrics.

Elongated Join

When just one row of very long double trebles is included between rows of double crochet, it is necessary to crochet the two long rows together for the seam in such a way that the join is not noticeable. Tall stitches do not sit tightly together in the same way as the shorter stitches, such as double crochet and half treble crochet.

After pinning the two pieces together, dc the denser parts of the design until the row of very tall sts is reached. Stretch the loop on the hook to exactly the height of the row of tall sts.

Insert the hook into the next row of shorter sts and continue to join with dc.

Should there be two rows of tall sts before returning to the denser fabric, insert the hook into the top of the last tall st in each piece, dc once and repeat Steps 2 and 3.

▲ The seam gives the illusion of continued spaces.

Other Uses

Other styles of crochet, such as broomstick and hairpin, benefit from using this technique.

Back Stitch Join

Select this method of joining when you need the seam to be very firm and immovable, as it is a stitch without elasticity.

When joining the tops of stitches together to form a seam, you can make a back stitch join on the right side. The tops of the two rows of stitches will stand up to form a design line.

Joining on the right side with a back stitch along the length of the stitches frequently looks unattractive and unless you need to form a picture with the back stitch seam, it is better to use this join on the wrong side.

Pin the two pieces together. Using the same yarn as the crochet item, bring the needle from the back to the front. Insert the needle backward from where it emerged. Take the needle behind the first point, bringing it out at a point in front of where you began.

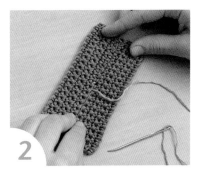

Repeat Step 1 to the end of the seam. Using the same yarn colour as the crochet, the back st seam is an invisible seam. Here a contrast yarn was used for clarity.

Whip Stitch

Whip stitch is also known as whipping stitch, oversewing and overcast stitch. This seam is one that lies flat (when the precautions of matching stitches and rows have been observed); it is also invisible. There is a tiny bit of elasticity in this method of sewing, but it is very limited.

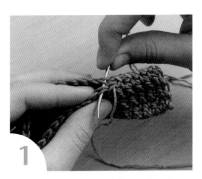

Pin the two pieces together. Using the same yarn as the crochet item, bring the needle from the back to the front. Repeat, allowing the yarn to go over the top of the two seams.

Continue to the end of the seam. Here a contrast yarn was used for clarity.

Mattress Stitch

The amount of elasticity in this stitch is similar to that of whip stitch. It makes an invisible seam, worked with the two edges lying side by side rather than being pinned together. I have found the mattress stitch suitable for double and treble crochet, but not for the taller stitches. As with all methods and techniques, this is only a guideline. Do be creative and experiment for yourself.

Take one of the crochet pieces and bring the needle from back to front. Leave 10cm (4in) yarn to close the seam. Take the yarn across to the other piece of crochet in the same place and push the needle from back to front. Leave the space open at the corresponding point. Thread the yarn through the st. For a dc use the whole st; for a tr use half the st. Take the needle across to the other crochet piece at the corresponding point. Continue to move from side to side, weaving the yarn through the sts. After working a few sts, pull the yarn in the needle and the starting yarn. This tightens the sts, making the seam invisible. Repeat to the end of the seam.

Mattress st makes an invisible seam when the same colour yarn as the crochet pieces is used. Here a contrast yarn was used for clarity.

Removing Fullness

Sometimes you will want to remove fullness from a garment and there are a few ways of doing this.

Pleating Crochet

There are not many occasions when it is right to pleat crochet. Two of them are maternity wear (made in yarn or thread) and designs in fine thread. One or two pleats, strategically placed, can hide a disproportionate figure. Ensure the pleats are secure and will not move by using slip stitches.

▲ Fold the crochet into pleats and pin. Work slip stitches through all three stitches, picking up six strands of yarn before working the slip stitch. Return with a row of double crochet before continuing in pattern.

Gathering Crochet

Gathering crochet into a band
is simple and effective. The most
common places gathering is used
are when making a cuff from a full
sleeve, working the fullness of a
hat into a headband, in maternity
wear, and also in designs based on
historical costume shapes such as
the leg-of-mutton sleeve or gigot
sleeve.

Work the crochet to the point where it is necessary to decrease for gathers. In double crochet, decrease two stitches together along the whole row. For fewer gathers, *work one stitch individually and then two stitches together for a decrease; rep from * across. Work next row in pattern without decreases.

Lining

Crochet rarely requires a lining. Now and again you may prefer to add
a lining to a garment either because you feel a skirt will hang better, or
the design of the crochet will show better over a block of colour. The
following points will help you to decide what to line and the best way
to do so.

Skirts	The lining of a skirt needs to be full enough to allow easy movement. Attach the lining only at the waistband. Connecting the skirt lining to any other part can distort the crochet and is usually uncomfortable to wear.
Jackets and Coats	I favour a loose lining that is attached at the top of the cuff on the inside of the sleeve and at the shoulder seams. The front edge should be sewn to the button and buttonhole bands, leaving the hem loose.
Lace Designs	Occasionally a lace design may require a strong contrasting colour beneath the item to accentuate the pattern. If this is the reason you choose to line a garment, make the lining to fit in every detail and then attach the crochet to the lining.
Iron-On Interfacing	Pictorial panels in crochet garments may benefit from being supported by iron-on interfacing. Pin it to the wrong side of the panel with the adhesive side down and with enough additional material to allow the interfacing to be turned under to form a neat hem after pressing. Press a hot iron on the interfacing just long enough to melt the glue but not so long as to distort the crocheted fabric. Leave the glue to cool and set before turning in the edges. With either a mattress stitch or a whip stitch, sew the edges of the interfacing to the crocheted panel.

Cuffs, Bands, Edgings and Pockets

The visual impact of any garment is accentuated by the cuffs, bands, edgings and pockets selected and added by the designer. When correctly placed and worked, they are a major contributor to a good design and create a professional finished look.

4

Finishing Touches

Cuffs, bands, edgings and pockets should blend smoothly into the design. An onlooker's eye should not be drawn to any of these features because of a substandard finish. Fortunately, there are many different ways to make and attach these items professionally.

Ribs for Welt, Neck and Cuffs

Working into the back loop of double crochet stitches, picking up only one strand instead of the usual two, produces a very effective rib. It is necessary to work the double crochet rib separately. It is either seamed to the main body of the work, or the main body of the work can be crocheted along the side edge of the ribbing in the row ends.

Double Crochet Rib

The rib is worked in narrow strips, inserting the hook into the back loop of one double crochet. Depending on the yarn selected, it may be necessary to reduce the size of the crochet hook in order to increase the elasticity of the rib. These narrow strips are then placed sideways around the wrist for a cuff, around the bottom of a sweater for a bottom rib or around the neck opening of the sweater for a neck band.

Keeping the edges straight on double crochet rib can be troublesome. By turning the crochet on each row toward you, like you would turn the page of a book (the opposite way to which I normally recommend the work be turned), then ch1, skipping first dc, working 1 dc in the second dc of the row, there will be no problem with the shape of the edges. The last stitch should be placed into what looks like a little knot at the end of the row – the turning ch of the row below.

1 Make a length of ch one more than the number of dc required for the rib.

2 Starting in 2nd ch from hook, work 1 dc into each ch across, turn.

3 Ch1 (counts as first dc), skip first ch and first dc, work 1 dc in the back loop of the next dc (resembles third ch top down from hook), 1 dc in back loop of each st across, ch1, turn.

▲ A section of completed double crochet rib.

Post Stitch Rib

A fabric made by using alternate front and back post stitches creates a very 'elastic' rib that is ideal for bottom ribs, cuffs and neck bands. As the number of rows worked increases, the elastic effect becomes stronger. This characteristic makes it very suitable for polo neck sweaters.

Seam the back and fronts together prior to starting the bottom rib. Please note that unless the post stitch rib is turned on every round, it will be a textured stitch and not an elastic post stitch rib. To counteract this, at the end of each round, join with a slip stitch, ch2, turn and continue keeping the post stitches in vertical rows.

1

For front post st, insert the hook to the right of the st, placing the stem of the st on the hook and emerging at the left of the st. Complete the st as normal.

2

For back post st, insert the hook to the right of the st, but from the back of the crochet.

3

Place the stem of the st on the hook and emerge to the left of the st at the back of the work. Complete the st as normal.

◀ The first row of treble crochet worked into the chain is not elastic, so all the post stitch ribs should be worked outward, away from the main fabric. Note that because the hook is inserted lower down the stitch to create a post stitch, the stitches will be shorter and require a shorter turning chain.

Bands

Bands can be purely a functional part of a design when worked using the same yarn and same hook as for the garment, and in simple stitches such as a double crochet. Alternatively, bands can form the main design feature, using colour and even a stitch variation to draw the eye.

Double Crochet Band

The first row of any band is the critical one. The stitches should be inserted in such a way that rows of previously crocheted stitches do not curve or distort but lie either horizontally, vertically or in line with the stitch design. Start by working the first row with the right side facing.

There is a guideline for knowing how many stitches are required on the first row. Obviously, when working a border at the top or bottom of a piece of crochet, it is stitch for stitch. Along the sides of the rows of crochet, it is necessary to place three double crochet stitches to every four rows of double crochet. In half treble crochet, place one double crochet to each row. For treble crochet, place three double crochet to two rows of treble crochet. For double trebles, two double crochets per row are required.

When a crochet band goes all around a piece of crochet, it is important to join the round with a slip stitch, chain one and turn the work before continuing to crochet the band. If this is not done, the next row of the band will not lie flat. Two further rows or rounds of double crochet (making three in all) leaves you with the right side facing. To remove the chain, look on the top of the last row, finish the band with a row or round of crab stitch. This produces a decorative finished edge.

▲ Three double crochet are required at the side of four double crochet rows to ensure that the band lies flat.

▲ Three double crochet are required at the side of two treble crochet rows to ensure that the band lies flat.

Right or Wrong Side?

The first row or round of a band in double crochet looks neater if worked on the right side. The only time to change this is if you have an even number of double crochet rows in the band, to prevent the last row of crab stitch being on the wrong side.

Button Band and Buttonhole Band

I am a great believer in working with odd numbers, particularly when adding no more than nine buttons. Sometimes an excellent jacket can look somehow out of balance because it has an even number of buttons.

Work the button band first. This gives the exact number of double crochet required for the first row. On the button band, mark the place for the top button and for the bottom button. With a tape measure, check how many more buttons are required. Carefully mark the button positions.

Buttonhole Row

Decide on the size of the button to be used. (Ideally, have an actual button in hand before working the buttonhole row on the buttonhole band.)

The buttonhole row will be the second row in a three-row buttonhole band, the third row in a five-row buttonhole band, or the fifth row in a seven-row buttonhole band. No, I have not miscounted. The wider the button and buttonhole band become, the closer to the edge of the buttonhole band the buttonhole row has to be placed.

Place one double crochet in each stitch to the marker. Skip one stitch. Replace with one chain. Continue in double crochet to the next marker and make another buttonhole. Try pushing the button through the buttonhole you have just made. If it is a struggle to get the button through it, skip two stitches and replace with two chains.

The next row of double crochet is worked with one double crochet in each stitch and one double crochet for each chain, placing the hook into the space beneath the chain, not into the chain itself.

Contrast Colour Band

Sometimes a band is the only design detail on a garment. Instead of working the first row into the top of all the stitches, insert the hook lower down in the fabric at regular intervals. This way of working a double crochet is often referred to as a spike stitch (see page 70). Working spike stitch makes the contrast band part of the design and not just another colour added as an afterthought or because the yarn used in the main body of the work has run out.

▲ One row of evenly spaced spike stitches instead of the traditional row of double crochet, followed by a row of crab stitch, creates an interesting border.

▲ The large-headed pins indicate the discreet buttonholes worked in the buttonhole band. The button band is alongside.

Alternative Use of Colour

A double crochet band of five rows can look very decorative when the alternate rows are worked in a contrast colour. Experiment with colours on your tension swatch before adding them to the garment itself.

Pockets

With the exception of an invisible pocket inserted in the side seam of a garment, pockets are a design feature. It is vital that extra care is taken to see they are worked and inserted with precision.

Patch Pockets

A patch pocket is one that is made to the size required and sewn into position at a later date. It can be fixed to a flat piece of crochet or sewn on after the whole garment has been assembled. I prefer to put the pocket on after the garment has been assembled, when I can get a complete overview of how the completed design will look.

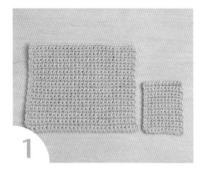

First of all, work the pocket (above right).

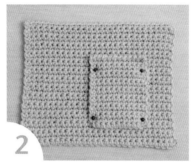

Once the position has been decided on, pin it in place and either oversew the edges with close whip sts or use a mattress st.

The sewn st should be close together. Lazy sewing – with the sewn sts lying apart from each other – means items can fall out of the pocket.

Pocket Inserted as the Garment is Constructed

Decide how large the opening of the pocket should be and work out the number of stitches needed to achieve the required width of opening. Count the number of stitches necessary prior to the opening for the pocket. Work up to these stitches, followed by the number of chains necessary to replace the stitches of the pocket. Continue in pattern across the row. Complete the garment.

▲ Opening for a pocket worked in the fabric. This is now ready for a pocket lining and border.

Pocket Lining

1 Make the pocket lining by joining the yarn to the ch worked to make the pocket opening, ch1, and place 1 dc in each of the chs made for the pocket opening. They are the chs that have already been used for the body of the garment.

2 Continue on these sts until the depth of the pocket has been reached. Fasten off.

3 Sew the side of the pocket lining to the inside of the garment.

Pocket Band

With the right side facing, rejoin the yarn to the first stitch of the pocket opening on the front. Ch1 and place 1 dc in each unworked stitch. Continue with two rows of dc on these stitches. Complete the pocket band with one row of crab stitch. Sew the sides of pocket band to front of sweater.

Practicalities

Pockets can be used on a practical level and also as a design feature. Try adding them into designs in unusual and quirky ways to set them off with a pop!

▲ Showing the pocket band ready for securing to the garment.

Invisible Side Pockets

This kind of pocket works well in a design with side seams. Although it is advised the fronts and back of a garment are worked together to avoid side seams, when a garment is worked from side to side or side to centre, seaming is inevitable. In such a situation side pockets can be inserted easily. The method of inserting a side pocket is described in detail on page 100 in the Cosy Jumper pattern.

▲ Detail showing the pocket pulled out from inside the jumper.

▲ Detail showing the pocket open.

Edgings

Designs with angles in the stitches or garment shape need crisp edgings without curves. Designs with scallop, fan or shell-type stitch structures and curved edges, require a softer edge such as a shell or picot edge.

Crab Stitch Edge

Crab stitches are worked from left to right (if you are right-handed) on the right side of the crochet as an edging or finishing row. A hook one size smaller than the one for the main fabric can make this stitch more attractive. It is not necessary to work a turning chain if the crab stitches are going to be worked in the round, but when working in rows, do chain 1 to raise the hook to the right height for a double crochet.

To make a crab st, working from left to right, insert the hook in next st on the right, through two strands of yarn as normal, then pick up the yarn from the ball by dropping the hook head onto the yarn as shown.

Bring the yarn through to the front of the work, tilting the hook upward.

Twist the hook to a normal working position, checking there are two loops on the hook. If you do not do this, you may draw the yarn through all the loops on the hook, thus creating a sl st.

Yo, draw through the two loops on the hook – and you have made one crab st.

▲ A crab stitch edge (shown at the base of this example) removes the chain look of the stitches, giving a professional finish.

Crab Stitch Edge for Round Items

If you place a crab stitch edge on anything that is worked in the round, whether it is a motif or a band going round the whole of a vest, the last stitch should not be worked. Instead, the knot created by fastening the yarn off will fill the gap.

1 Stop working the crab st one st before the round is completed.

2 Fasten off in the normal way.

3 Thread yarn into a tapestry needle. The knot created by fastening off the yarn lies over the skipped st.

▲ A neat finish.

Shell Edge

A shell edge is suitable for dainty pieces of crochet, whether for household items, items for children or on delicate thread or lacy designs. Avoid working a shell edge where the main stitch pattern is geometrically angular and contains no curves – a crisp, angular look does not blend well with a shell stitch edge.

The stitches needed to work a shell edge should be divisible by 6 plus 1. Join the yarn to the end stitch without any turning or lifting chain worked.

1 *Skip next 2 sts, 5 tr in next st.

2 Picture shows completing the 5 tr.

3 Skip next 2 tr, 1 dc in next st; rep from * to end.

▲ The finished shell edge.

Picot

Picots are little 'lumps' or 'blips' added to open fabrics and edges to remove a linear look. These are achieved by working a few chain stitches, which are then anchored with either a slip stitch or a double crochet into the first chain made. Occasionally, the pattern may suggest the chains are anchored into the previous stitch made. The number of chains needed may fluctuate and the number of stitches between picots can vary.

*Make 3 ch.

Make 1 sl st in first of 3 ch just worked.

Insert hook in next st.

Work a dc.

Make 1 dc in next st in readiness for another picot.

▲ The finished picot edge.

An Edging for all Seasons

Some borders create curved edges only suitable for delicate or lacy designs while others create sharp angles better suited to angular designs. The picot edge is a slightly textured and more versatile edging that can be used to accent almost any kind of crocheted fabric, whether angular or rounded.

Half Treble Crochet Puff Slitch Edge

The half treble crochet is just tall enough to allow puff stitches to be worked around it. These then lie sideways to give an interesting edge to any classic lines or fabrics that have angular stitches as part of their design. To accentuate the puff stitch as a design feature, it is possible to work the htr sideways puff in a different colour. Finish with one row crab stitch in the main colour. Work 1–3 rows double crochet as a base for the edging. Ensure that the number of stitches on the edge is an even number.

1 Ch2, *1 htr in next st.

2 Yo, insert the hook in the space behind the htr just made.

3 Yo, draw the loop up to 1cm (½in) three times, yo.

4 Draw yarn through all seven loops on hook, skip 1 st.

5 Rep from * to end, placing 1 htr in last st.

Design Flair

The half double crochet puff stitch edge can be adapted as part of a design feature in a crochet fabric. This would look stylish along the bottom of a skirt or edge of a jumper, to suggest only a few.

▲ The finished half treble crochet puff stitch edge.

Creative Use of Half Treble Crochet

The fascinating characteristic of htr is the way it ends with three horizontal strands of yarn to be creative with, instead of the usual two. This makes it ideal for very imaginative and colourful edgings. The one shown here is very basic, but you can let your imagination roam and use a variety of stitches and colours. This edge is particularly useful as an addition to a fairly simple design. Work the border or edge to the depth required and with the last row a htr. Identify the three strands.

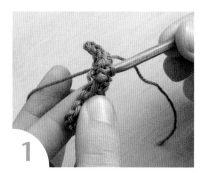

With the right side facing, work 1 dc in each st, using the lowest front strand.

With the right side facing, working in the strand that is farthest away at the back of the htr, work 1 tr in each st.

This leaves one strand of yarn between the two rows now worked. With right side facing, join yarn in centre strand of first htr on the left, ch1, crab st in the centre of the two rows using the remaining strand of yarn from the original htr.

▲ There are three different rows of stitches to form an interesting edge, worked into the three strands left at the top of each stitch in the half treble crochet row.

Using Colour

There is a magical magnetism to colour.
Good design combines colour with yarn
and stitches in balanced and appealing
ways. Include colour in the construction
of the crochet fabric, within an edging
or as an embellishment.

5

Colour Know-How

Colour is a matter of personal choice. From the very bright mixtures of the tropics, to the muted and misty looks of the Scottish Highlands, there is a wealth of plain colours, blends and combinations to select from. Often it is the colour of an article that attracts the eye and therefore it is important that any changes of colour in an item are worked in such a way that they are not noticeable.

Preventing Colour Drag

Crochet begins and ends with one loop on the hook. When the turning chains are made, the first of those chains is in the old colour, creating a colour drag. When introducing a new colour, the way to avoid this is to work the last stitch prior to incorporating the new colour until there are two loops on the hook. Draw the new yarn through the last two loops of the stitch so the loop on the hook is already in the new colour and is ready for the next stitch pattern. Use this method when working stripes of colour, so the beginning of the rows contain the new colour in the turning chains and there is no colour drag.

1 This picture shows the colour drag.

2 Prevent colour drag by working the new colour to finish the last st.

Colour or Texture?

It is worth practicing any stitch pattern where the hook is inserted in row(s) below the top of the stitches. If the stitches are too loose, they can catch when worked. If the stitches are too tight, the foundation fabric will curl and pucker instead of remaining flat.

Hiding a Colour in Two-Row Stripes

The varying heights of stitches can be a problem. Carrying colours up the side of the work creates floats or carried strands, that can either be left loose and are then liable to be caught in wear or can be worked over with a border. The problem with the latter method is that the yarn being worked over will change the look of the colour of the first row of the border. I would advise you to cut the yarn for any design where the stripes are deeper than two rows of double treble. Try to link the yarn into a stitch along the side if possible.

Changing Colour on Every Row

As there is only one loop on a crochet hook, the hook can be inserted anywhere within the fabric and you do not need to turn the work on every row. When using two colours of yarn, changing on every row, the work can be turned on every other row and both yarns can stay attached without colour drag or floats. Understanding the points given here makes it easier to work these rows.

Key Notes for Changing Colour on Every Row	
	1. Unlike other textiles, the stitches in crochet do not lie precisely on top of each other. Turning on every row, right-handed workers insert the hook to the left of the stitch, and left-handed crocheters insert it to the right of the stitch. There are very few stitches where the hook is inserted into the centre of the stitch.
	2. On the row that starts with the work being turned, the hook is inserted in the usual way. On the row where the work is not turned, right-handed workers need to put the hook to the right of the stitch and left-handed people need to put it to the left of the stitch.
	3. The loop that is left at the end of a row waiting for the next row to be completed needs to be secured in a safety pin or row marker to prevent the work from unravelling.
	4. Once the loop in the pin has been reached, it is important to place the loop on the hook after the hook has been inserted into the last stitch of the row. This ensures that the work is secure. The stitch is then worked in the colour of the row until two loops remain. The colour that was held in the pin is then used to complete the last stitch.
	5. Count the stitches on every row to ensure that you have not missed one during the colour changes.

1 Without turning the work, collect the yarn at the beginning of the row.

2 Insert the hook to the right of the st at the beginning of the row.

3 At the end of that row, insert the hook in the last st containing the safety pin.

4 Place the loop from the safety pin onto the hook.

5 With the working yarn, pull through the loop from the pin and from the st.

6 Work the st until only two loops are left on the hook; change yarn to complete the st.

◀ Work ready to turn for the next row.

Before You Start

Before embarking on a large project such as the jumper on page 100, work the following test piece for confidence in using this process.

With first colour, ch17.

Row 1: 1 tr in 4th ch from hook, 1 tr in each ch to the end, changing to second colour in the last st. (15 sts)

Row 2: With the second colour, ch1, *1 dtr in next st, 1 dc in next st; rep from * to end. Leave the last loop in a holder. Do not turn the work. This is the wrong side of the fabric.

Row 3: With wrong side facing, pick up first colour from 2 rows below, hook in the first stitch of the row that is the turning chain, ch3, inserting the hook to the right of the next stitch work 1 tr, tr each st across to the last st, yo, inserting the hook into the last st, pick up the loop from the holder from two rows below, work the stitch until two loops remain, completing the st with the new colour. Turn work.

Row 4: With right side facing, ch1, work same as row 2 pulling the loops made by the dtr stitches toward you, leaving last loop in holder. This is the front of the fabric. Do not turn.

Row 5: With right side facing, work same as row 3.

Repeat the last four rows until you feel confident with the process.

▲ The completed piece, with colour sucessfully changed on every row.

Using More Than One Colour in a Row

Designs with more than one colour in the row ideally need to have the yarns not in use carried and twisted around each other at every stitch, or every other stitch, to avoid yarn floats at the back of the work which may catch during wear. As with all colour changes, it is necessary to work the stitch prior to the change taking place until there are two loops on the hook. Finish the stitch with the new colour.

Sometimes it is possible to work over the yarn not in use, allowing the colour to show through the stitches and giving a shadow effect to the fabric – but in most cases carrying the yarn in this manner produces an unattractive effect. Use it only when you want the effect as a design feature.

1

In the middle of a row, work the last colour until two loops remain.

2

After working a st, twist the colour not in use around the yarn of the colour in use.

3

The length of thread being carried is now shortened. The work is ready to change the colour again.

▲ There is no bleeding of colour in these diagonal stripes.

Escapees

Once you are feeling confident about using more than one colour, you may forget to check whether the wrong colour is showing on the right side. Check frequently – it is better to be safe than sorry, if the error is later you may need to tear out many rows to correct it.

Working with Blocks of Colour

Irregularly shaped blocks of colour can be worked individually. The second and subsequent blocks of colour link into the sides of any crochet rows previously worked. The connecting link does not need to be a crochet stitch. Instead, remove the loop on the hook and pull through the stitch to which it needs to be linked. Tall stitches may require more than one connecting link. For instance, in a block of colour containing a row of taller stitches such as double trebles, it may be necessary to work a turning chain. If more than two chains are required, link every other chain into the block of colour. This prevents ugly holes in fabrics of solid colour.

1 At the end of the row in a block of colour, complete the last st.

2 Remove the hook from the loop and insert the hook into the side of the st, where the block of colour being crocheted is to be joined to a block of colour already worked.

3 Pull the loop just removed from the hook through the fabric, turn work and continue to crochet the current block of colour.

4 Where the present colour has to be connected to another block of colour, work sufficient chain to lift the hook to the height of the next row.

5 Remove the loop from the hook, inserting the hook into the top of the row of the block of colour previously worked.

6 Pull the loop through to link the two blocks of colour together.

7 Continue working the row.

Camouflaging Stripes of Colour

There are three main ways to camouflage colour using a crochet hook. Each one is simple. It is often true that an extremely simple technique has far more versatility than a complex technique.

Ways to Camouflage Stripes of Colour	1. Should you be experimenting with blocks of colour for a pictorial panel and when the panel is complete you feel that some of the colours do not go well together, you can simply dye the panel. A light colour bath will merge into all the colours present, giving an over-colour rather like a thin film of dust. The effect will dim the brighter colours, giving a complementary shadow throughout the panel. This will soften the displeasing bright contrasts.
	2. If you know there are some yarn colours that do not mingle well, take a thin complementary thread and work this with the yarn. The two threads will automatically ply themselves as they are crocheted and the complementary thread will soften the harsher colours. If you are using textured yarn that is exactly the texture you want but not the colour, this technique of adding a smooth yarn can be very rewarding.
	3. Work tambour surface crochet either from the back to the front for a small amount of detail or from the front to the back to allow more yarn to cover and float over the area needing to be camouflaged. Surface crochet breaks up blocks of colour, helping the whole to intermingle (see page 90).
	4. If a large block of colour displeases you, it is possible to add three-dimensional surface crochet (see page 91) or appliquéd motifs that have been worked separately. Lace motifs look delightful over blocks of strong colour, as the deep contrast shows through the holes of the motif.

Spike Stitches

Spike stitches are a double crochet placed two or more rows below your working row to create interesting edges and designs on fabrics.

1 Use a spike st in stripes of dc to create geometric designs.

2 Work a dc in the top of a st as usual.

3 Work the next dc through the row below.

4 Work carefully so the length of yarn lies snugly over the rows without distortion.

5 Work a third dc in the st two rows below; work a fourth dc in the st three rows below.

6 Continue with the spike st geometric design, changing colour at the end of the row to prevent colour drag.

Long Double Treble Post Stitches

Use long double treble post stitches to drop over a stripe of colour crochet.
This will break up the stripe into sections.

1 Place the post st around the top of the stitch of the row below the colour stripe you want to camouflage.

2 The two rows below of tr require a sextuple post st. Collect the yarn in readiness for working the sextuple post st.

3 Work the sextuple post st, taking care to control the loops so the stitch does not look ragged once complete.

4 Check that the st is the correct length and does not distort the crochet fabric.

5 Now you are ready to make the next st.

◀ A section worked using three separate colours for effect.

Creating Shapes

Decorative shapes in the form of
motifs or buttons can be used for
all kinds of embellishment as well as
having a functional capacity. Enjoy
being creative with the flowers
and trims in this chapter.

6

Shapes and Motifs

Symmetrical shapes are often worked from a circle in the centre. It is important to keep the shapes flat unless you are making a three-dimensional piece. The following points explain what to do if your work is curling into a saucer shape or has begun to frill.

Key Points to Consider when Creating Shapes

1. When working in the round, the bottom of a crochet stitch can be compressed with no ugly visual evidence. The top of a crochet stitch, however, is very noticeable. The chain look at the top of a stitch is the controlling factor for deciding how many stitches need to be placed into a ring for the shape to remain flat.

2. The way the stitch is constructed by the crocheter is the key to any motif or other crochet patterns. In Europe for instance, people lift the crochet hook at the point where the thread is brought through to the front. This elongates the stitches, making them taller than those worked by UK or US designers. If when following a pattern the work does not lie flat but begins to frill, elongate the stitches as they are worked. If the motif is turning into a concave shape, you will probably need to use a larger hook or increase the number of stitches in the round.

3. The height of the stitch determines how many stitches are needed to start a shape when working from the centre:
6 dc need to be placed in the ring with 6 dc increased on every round.
8 htr need to be put in the ring with 8 htr being increased on every round.
Start with 12 tr and increase 12 tr per round to keep tr rnds lying flat.

4. Even if the shape will eventually stretch to 1m (3ft) or more, the number of stitches increased on each round remains the same. It is not the size of the article but the size of the stitch that is the determining factor in deciding the number of increases.

5. When working in the round, I always advise people to turn the work on every round (unless the pattern indicates differently). If crochet is not turned on every round, it has a tendency to curl into a concave shape. When designing your own motifs, try to design them so they can be turned on each round. The only exception is a lace motif. (Patterns for lacy designs, which contain motifs, will have taken any curling effects into account during the design process.)

6. To make a true circle, it is necessary to stagger the place where the increases are being worked. If you put the increases in the same place, a double crochet circle will end up as a hexagon.

7. All rounds should be joined either with a slip stitch or by linking after removing the loop on the hook. Once joined, a turning or lifting chain is required.

8. Joins in each round should not be noticeable, therefore I suggest you take the loop off the hook and with one side facing, pull the loop from front to back. On the next round, if you have turned the work, take the loop off the hook and pull this from back to front; otherwise, repeat the action that looks the neatest in the shape you are creating.

Geometric Shapes

A few of the more usual geometric shapes have been explored here, but remember that there are many other shapes that can be worked and incorporated into designs – either as part of a crochet fabric or as an embellishment.

Circles

Triangles Worked to a Point

▲ A treble crochet triangle, worked in rows.

Work an odd number of chains to begin the triangle. Treble crochet triangles need to be decreased at both ends of every row. Decrease on every row, including the first row.

Row 1: Tr in 4th ch from hook (ch3 and tr count as first tr2tog), tr in each ch across to within last 2 ch, tr2tog in last 2 ch, turn.
Row 2: Ch3, tr in next st (count as first tr2tog), tr in each st across to within last 2 sts, tr2tog in last 2 sts, turn.
Rep Row 2 until 3 sts remain.
Last row: Ch3, tr2tog in last 2 sts.

Triangles Worked from a Point

▲ A treble crochet triangle.

To make a treble crochet triangle worked from a point:
Ch3 (unless your chains are very tight, in which case you should ch4).
Row 1: 2 tr in 1st ch from hook, turn.
Row 2: Ch3, tr in first tr (inc made), 2 tr in top of turning chain (inc made).
Row 3: Ch3, tr in first tr (inc made), tr in each tr across, 2 tr in top of turning chain (inc made).
Rep row 3 until triangle is as large as you want.

▲ Circles turn into spirals when the rows are not joined and the stitches are worked in the round continuously. This is only suitable if the stitch is short, as with the double crochet. Taller stitches leave an ugly step at the end of the first round.

Other Triangles

▲ A right-angled triangle: only one side has any increases or decreases and the other side remains straight.

▲ A triangle can begin in the centre of the hypotenuse (the long side of a right-angled triangle). This method is very useful when you need half granny squares to complete a larger project composed of granny squares. The triangle is increased in three places: at the beginning, middle and end of the row. The largest angle is created by the increase in the middle of the row.

▲ Triangles that are made from the centre can be isosceles or equilateral, depending on where you put the increases and how many increase stitches you incorporate.
Adding two stitches to each increase will give an equilateral triangle, whereas one stitch added in two corners and four stitches added in the third corner will give an isosceles triangle.

Diamonds

▲ Diamonds can be made by working an isosceles triangle from a point to midway in the diamond and then working another isosceles triangle to the point.

Hexagons

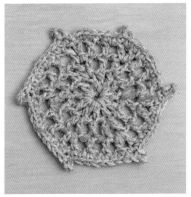

▲ Hexagons are mainly worked in double crochet and require the increases to be placed in the same place on every round. Between the increases there are straight rows of stitches. Other stitches can be included as they are here.

Squares

▲ A square such as a granny square usually has three additional stitches added to all four corners.

Octagons and Lacy Motifs

◀ Octagons are worked on a similar principle, but use half treble crochet stitches. Eight increases per round are required (far left). Lacy motifs are also popular and can be expanded for use as coasters, doilies or table centres (left).

Thread Crochet

Unlike yarn, which has some elasticity within the fibres, crochet thread is normally manufactured in cotton or linen. It is unforgiving and therefore the tension must be exact for every stitch. The tension for thread crochet is the same as for yarn when worked in rows. For any crochet that starts in the centre to make a motif or shape, the measure given for the tension will be across the diameter for a certain number of rounds.

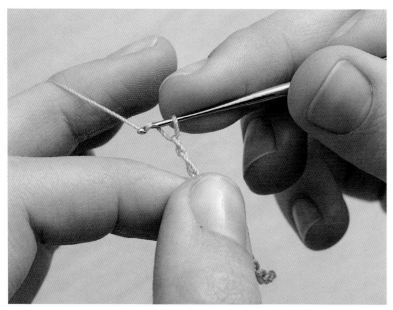

▲ Most steel hooks used for thread crochet are shaped like an embroiderer's tambour hook and require you to use another finger – you hold it on top of the hook to act as a stop.

Motifs

Any of the following lacy motifs can be worked in thread and appliquéd onto a surface. They have many uses: to camouflage colour, or as an embellishment to create an original design. They can also be used as part of a larger article or connected together to form a design. They make great coasters with one or two more added rounds. Most importantly, the designs can be worked in any thickness of thread or yarn, as long as the chosen hook is suitable for it.

Motif 1

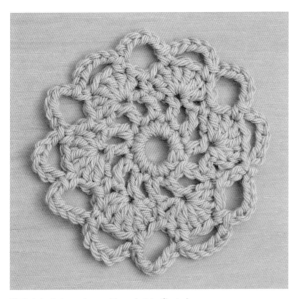

Ch8, join into a ring with a sl st in first ch.

Round 1: Ch1 (counts as first dc), 11 dc in centre of ring, sl st in first ch to join.

Round 2: Ch4 (counts as tr, ch1), *1 tr in next st, ch1; rep from * around, sl st to 3rd ch of turning ch.

Round 3: Ch1 (counts as first dc), *skip next ch-1 sp, 5 tr in next tr, skip next ch-1 sp, 1 dc in next tr; rep from * around, omitting last dc, sl st in first ch to join.

Round 4: Sl st in each of next 2 tr, *ch5, skip next tr, 1 dc in next tr, ch5, skip next 3 sts, 1 dc in next tr; rep from * around, omitting last dc, sl st in first ch to join. Fasten off.

Motif 2

Ch5, join into a ring with a sl st in first ch.

Round 1: Ch4 (counts as tr, ch1), *1 tr in ring, ch1; rep from * 10 times, sl st to 3rd of turning ch to join (12 ch-1 sp).

Round 2: Sl st in next ch-1 sp, ch3 (counts as first st of cluster), tr2tog in same place, ch2, tr3tog in next ch-1 sp, ch3, *1 dtr in next tr, ch3, (tr3tog in next ch sp, ch2) 3 times, ch1; rep from * twice, 1 dtr in next tr, ch3, tr3tog in next ch-1 sp, ch2, sl st in 3rd ch of turning ch.

Round 3: Ch3 (counts as first dc ch2), skip next ch-2 sp, *4 tr in next 3ch sp, ch2, 1 dtr in next dtr, ch2, 4 tr in next ch-3 sp, ch2, skip next ch-2 sp, 1 dc in next cluster, ch2; rep from * 3 times omitting the last dc and ch-2 sp, sl st in first ch to join. Fasten off.

Motif 3

Ch3, join into a ring with a sl st in first ch.

Round 1: Ch3 (counts as first st of cluster), tr2tog in ring to complete cluster, *ch3, tr3tog (cl) in ring; rep from * 4 times, ch1, 1 tr in top of first cl.

Round 2: Ch3 (counts as first st of cluster), tr2tog in same sp to complete cluster, *ch3, (1 cl, ch3, 1 cl) in next ch-3 sp; rep from * 4 times, work 1 cl in beg ch-sp, ch1, 1 tr in top of first cl.

Round 3: Ch3 (counts as first st of cluster), tr2tog in same sp to complete cluster, *ch3, (1 cl, ch3, 1 cl) in next ch-3 sp, ch3, 1 cl in next ch-3 sp, ch3; rep from * 4 times, ch3, (1 cl, ch3, 1 cl) in next ch-3 sp, ch3, sl st in top of first cl.

Round 4: Ch1 (counts as first dc), *3 dc in next ch-3 sp, 1 dc in next cl; rep from * around, omitting last dc, sl st in first ch to join. Fasten off.

Motif 4

Ch4, join into a ring with a sl st in first ch.

Round 1: Ch3 (counts as first tr), 11 tr in ring, join with sl st in 3rd ch of beg ch.

Round 2: Ch4 (counts as tr, ch1), *(1 tr, ch1, 1 tr) in next tr, ch1, tr in next tr, ch1; rep from * to end omitting last tr and ch, join with sl st in 3rd ch of beg ch.

Round 3: Sl st in first ch-1 sp, ch4 (counts as tr, ch1), *(1 tr, ch1, 1 tr) in next ch-1 sp, (1 tr, ch1) in each of next 2 ch-1 sp; rep * from to end, omitting last tr and ch1, join with sl st in 3rd ch of beg ch.

Round 4: Sl st to second ch-1 sp, ch1 (counts as first dc), *ch3, sl st in 3rd ch from hook (for picot), (1 dc in next tr, 1 dc in next ch-1 sp) 4 times; rep from * around, omitting last dc, sl st in first ch to join. Fasten off.

Motif 5

In first colour, ch6, join into a ring with a sl st in first ch.

Round 1: Ch1 (counts as first dc), 7 dc in ring, sl st in first ch to join.

Round 2: Ch3 (counts as first st of cl), tr2tog in first st to complete cluster, *ch3, tr3tog in next st; rep from * 6 times, ch3, sl st to top of first cl to join. Fasten off yarn.

Round 3: Join second colour in any ch-3 sp, ch4 (counts as dc, ch3), *1 tr in next cl, ch3, 1 dc in next ch-3 sp, ch3; rep from * around, omitting last dc and ch3, sl st to first of beg ch4. Fasten off second yarn.

Motifs as a Fabric

When four or more motifs are being put together it is better to join them while the last row of the motif is being constructed. The first motif needs to be made and fastened off. All subsequent motifs can then be joined using either the faggot join or, in the case of granny squares, a mock filet join.

Filler

When working a fabric composed of circle motifs, there will be unattractive gaps between the circles. For a very quick filler, start with ch4, join into a ring with a sl st in first ch. Keep this ring in the centre of the gap, *work a sufficient number of chains to connect the filler to a place on one of the circles, connect with dc, chain the same number to take you back to the ring of four chains, 1 dc in ring; rep from * evenly spacing the linking chains to suit the original design.

For the centre of the gap, make a ring of 4 ch joined with a sl st.

Make sufficient chs to carry the thread to a point on one of the motifs; join with dc.

Work the same number of chs and connect to the ring with 1 dc.

Continue working lengths of chs in this way, connecting with dc until the gap has been filled.

▲ The last connection needs to be in the starting ring of the filler.

Trims

Use simple finishing touches to customise your work. A crocheted button, tassel, fringe or plait can add colour or give your piece an air of classic design. Sometimes it is hard to purchase exactly the right trimmings for a project. The solution to this is to make your own – you can tailor size, colour and texture to your requirements.

Buttons

Buttons are quick and easy to make and I have included a selection of five for you to experiment with. Each is worked over a different filling. You can have fun trying out different yarns and threads for the designs.

   Below are some points that need to be taken into consideration when making buttons to ensure professional and durable results.

Creating Buttons	
	1. Work directly into the slip knot as described when the short or tail end of the yarn is the one that tightens on the hook.
	2. Place all of the first round of stitches directly under one strand of the slip knot, checking that it will tighten when the tail end is pulled up.
	3. Ensure that the casing is no larger than the object it is covering, whether that is a bead, ring, button or mould. If anything, it should be slightly smaller to ensure the casing fits tightly around the filling.
	4. Use the same yarn as the garment you are matching, but change to a smaller hook to crochet the buttons.
	5. Leave enough depth behind the button to form a shank. It is easy to attach a button too close to the band, meaning that there is insufficient room for the buttonhole fabric to sit neatly behind it.
	6. When using old buttons or beads as a base, their colour may shine through the crochet. If the colours are complementary, it doesn't matter, but if you are using odd buttons the variation in colour could make a difference. Sometimes the buttons look dirty. To rectify these problems, glue a tiny piece of the fabric to each button with fabric glue, so the buttons will look the same through the crocheted casings.

Button 1

Round 1: Ch2 (counts as first dc), work 6 dc into the top strand of the slip knot, join with a sl st in top of ch2. (7 sts)

Round 2: Ch1 (counts as first dc), 1 dc in same place, 2 dc in each sc around, do not join, work in a spiral.

Round 3: *Dc2tog in next 2 sts*; rep from * to * around, inserting the button before the hole is completely closed, but when the hole can take the button. Continue, rep from * to * until the hole is closed. Fasten off, leaving a long enough length of yarn to attach to the garment.

Button 2

Round 1: Ch3, work 8 tr into the top strand of the slip knot, join with a sl st to top of beg ch3, do not join, work in a spiral.

Round 2: *Tr2tog in next 2 sts*; rep from * to * around, inserting the button before the hole is completely closed, but when the hole can take the button being covered. Continue, rep from * to * until the hole is closed. Fasten off, leaving a long enough length of yarn to attach to the garment.

Button 2 can be filled with its own yarn, but it is essential to push sufficient yarn firmly into the casing to ensure that it does not become soft during wear.

Button 3

Working over a plastic ring, insert the hook into the space in the centre of the ring, dc all around the ring until the tops of the sts sit comfortably side by side without fullness and without spaces. Join with a sl st in first dc, leaving a long length of thread. Using a suitable size tapestry needle, sew four tight lines from the bottom of the sts across the ring centre to give eight spokes. With a separate strand of yarn, using a yarn needle and commencing at the point where the threads cross, *weave over one strand, under one strand; rep from * 3 times, working one time over two spokes to fill in the centre space. Use remaining yarn to make a shank to attach to the garment.

Button 4

Button 5

For this button you need a button mould.

Round 1: With the first colour, ch4, (1 tr, ch1) 8 times in the slip knot, sl st in 3rd ch of beg ch4. Fasten off.

Round 2: Join the second colour in any ch-1 sp, ch1 (counts as first dc), 1 dc in same sp, 2 dc in each ch-1 sp around, sl st in first ch to join.

Round 3: Ch2, *tr2tog over next 2 sts*, rep from * to * around, but do not join into a round. Insert the mould into the casing and continue, rep from * to * around until the hole is filled. Fasten off, leaving enough yarn to make a shank to attach the button to the garment.

Have a square button or square piece of wood available for the filling. Use thread rather than yarn. Chain as many stitches as needed to wrap fully around the top, sides and back of the square button.

Row 1: 1 dc in 2nd ch from hook, dc in each ch across, turn.

Row 2: Ch1, skip first dc, dc in each dc across, dc in turning ch, turn.

Rep row 2 for pattern, working one more row with first colour, then work one or two rows in each remaining colour, creating a symmetrical pattern. Finish with three rows of dc worked in the first colour. Fasten off, leaving sufficient thread to join the two edges together down the centre back of the button and at one of the ends. Insert the button into the casing. Carry the last thread used for sewing the button in place to the centre back of the button. Form a shank with this thread, ready to attach the button to the garment.

Plaits

Plaits should have both edges the same and it is the one time when a purl edge rather than a straight edge is recommended.

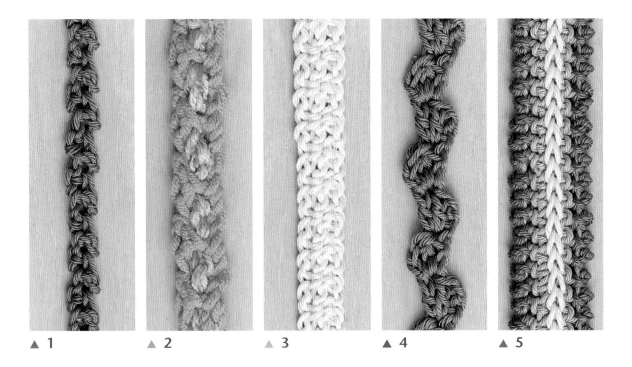

▲ 1   ▲ 2   ▲ 3   ▲ 4   ▲ 5

Plait 1

Ch2, 1 dc in 2nd ch from hook, *turn work, ch2, 1 dc in next dc; rep from * to length required.

Plait 2

First make a length of Plait 1. With a very thick and contrasting yarn, make a chain longer than the length of the Plait 1 worked. Thread this chain through the centre of the plait.

Plait 3

Ch4, 1 dc in 3rd ch from hook, 1 dc in last ch, *ch2, turn work, 1 dc in first dc, 1 dc in next dc; rep from * to length required.

Plait 4

Ch3, 2 tr in 3rd ch from hook, turn, *ch3, 2 tr in first tr, turn; rep from * to length required.

Plait 5

This three-colour plait is different, needing a starting chain the length of the required plait, using the central colour. With first colour, make a ch of desired length for plait.

Row 1: Starting in 2nd ch from hook, work 1 dc in top loop of each ch across, 3 dc in last ch, working across opposite side of foundation ch, 1 dc in one loop only of each ch across, leaving one strand unworked. Fasten off 1st colour.

In the colour selected for the outside of the plait, join yarn in last dc of row 1, ch1, work one crab st in each dc along both sides of row 1. Fasten off 2nd colour.

Starting at bottom of plait, with the final colour, work tambour surface crochet, placing the hook in each st over the remaining strand of the foundation chain. Refer to page 90 for this technique.

Twisted Cord

Occasionally it is necessary to thread a ribbon or cord through a crocheted piece. The twisted cord is the simplest of all to produce and once finished, gives a pleasing result.

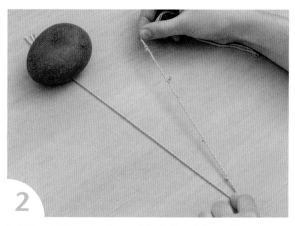

Cut lengths of yarn that are three times as long as the desired finished cord. Use two or more long strands of yarn and knot them at one end. Secure this knot over a nail, chair leg, door knob or under a heavy object. Twist the threads until they are so tight they want to curl in on themselves.

Fold the tightly twisted strands in half and they will automatically twist as one cord. Knot the two ends together and decorate with a tassel or sew the ends into beads.

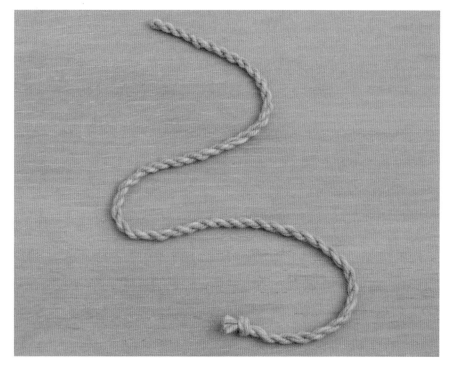

◀ The twisted cord can be made in the same colour as the article, but using different colours of yarn can add an interesting design detail.

Fringing

Decide on the length of the fringing and for each tuft of the fringe, cut two to four lengths of yarn measuring just over twice that length. The more strands you cut, the thicker the fringe will be.

1

Fold the strands in half. Insert the hook into the place you want to put the fringe and use it to pull the folded yarn through part of the way.

2

Pull the cut ends through the folded end and pull on the ends to tighten the fringe. Repeat to make each tuft of the fringe, working along the garment.

◀ For a longer fringe, it is possible to add a further decorative element. Taking half the strands from one tuft and half from another tuft, knot the group together in an overhand knot. Repeat across the entire fringed edge. If the fringe is a long one, a second row of overhand knots can be worked.

Tassels

To make a simple tassel, you need a piece of stiff cardboard or other rigid material the size of the finished length of the tassel. Check first to make sure that the yarn ball has enough yarn left on it to make the size and shape tassel you require. Be creative and use different coloured yarns to make a series of tassels; this will add an interesting, original edge to your project. Children usually find helping make tassels fun and get to see the results, fast.

1

Wrap the yarn around a piece of stiff cardboard until it is as thick as required.

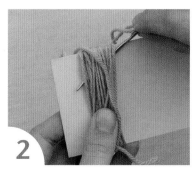

2

Secure the loops prior to removing them from the cardboard.

3

Wrap the yarn tightly around one end several times, then secure by sewing the end through all the loops. Cut the ends of the tassel.

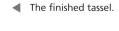 The finished tassel.

Embellishments

Previous sections have included embellishments such as plaits, buttons, motifs, colour camouflage, etc. Adding beads and sequins, making flowers for a corsage and surface crochet are three additional techniques that can be used to enhance a design.

Beads and Sequins

Large beads and sequins can be appliquéd onto the work using a sewing needle, but it is fun to incorporate small beads and sequins as you work.

1. Thread the beads or sequins onto the yarn or thread. If the hole in the beads is very small, thread them onto a fine sewing cotton in a matching colour and crochet both strands together as though they were one plied yarn, drawing up each bead as desired.

2. Slide the bead or sequin into the work at the point you need to place it. Do check that it is lying on the right side of the work. Beads and sequins have a habit of going to the wrong side of the fabric.

To check which side the bead will emerge, work a swatch and determine for yourself if the bead is best placed in position before or after the stitch is constructed. There is no absolute guideline for this as the type of yarn or thread being used plays a prominent part in deciding where the bead will lie in the stitch of your choice.

3. Where it is difficult to use a sewing needle when threading the beads onto yarn, dip the end of the yarn into a fabric glue such as one with a latex base. Shape this into a point and thread the yarn directly through the holes in the beads.

Surface Crochet

There are two types of surface crochet, the Tambour Method and Three Dimensional Crochet.

Tambour Method

The tambour method of surface crochet is one that is borrowed from embroidery: the yarn is placed beneath the work and the hook is inserted from the top.

Make a slip knot and place it behind the crocheted fabric. Insert hook through fabric and draw slip knot through to front of work.

*Insert hook approximately 1cm (½ in) away, yarn over from the back and draw yarn through fabric and loop on the hook. Repeat from * for desired length of surface crochet.

◄ To make a picture panel in a garment, do a rough sketch of what is to be added after the base has been made. This allows you to plan all the yarns you need ahead of time.

Of course, you still have the option of adding little bits and pieces later, after the bulk of the surface work has been done.

Three-Dimensional Crochet

Three-dimensional crochet can be achieved by having both the hook and the yarn on top of the crochet fabric. The method of working is exactly as you would crochet a row of textured stitches such as clusters, popcorns, pom-poms, shells and post stitches in a crochet fabric for a garment. The difference is that these textured stitches are worked into a fold of the crochet fabric and not into the stitch tops. Once one section or one 'row' of crochet has been worked, it is possible to come back on top of the stitches to create an even deeper texture.

The choice of colour and yarn can detract from or enhance the work, so please experiment first. Experimentation is not only fun, but a must when producing bigger projects using expensive materials. It gives you a chance to use unusual yarns in an enjoyable and creative way.

Insert the hook through the spaces at the side of a st and pull the yarn through ready for working the three-dimensional surface crochet.

Fold the base fabric along the line on which you wish to insert crochet sts and continue with the design.

Many sts can be put into the same place, but then a short length of chain may be required to carry the hook and the yarn to the next point.

Flowers

Flowers can be made in any yarn or thread and therefore I have not recommended a hook size, thread or yarn for making the four simple flowers on these pages. Make them in fine thread to enhance a wedding dress or with chunky yarn to embellish a tote bag or for producing theatrical props.

Buttercup

This is a simple, quick-to-make flower motif. Scatter several of them across a throw or the yoke of a garment – it can look very modern in a fun way.

With yellow, ch4, join into a ring with 1 sl st in first ch.
Round 1 (RS): No chain needs to be made. (1 dc, ch2) 5 times in ring, sl st in first dc to join.
Round 2: *In next ch-2 sp work (1 dc, 2 tr, tr3tog, 2 tr, 1 dc); rep from * 4 times, sl st in first dc to join (5 petals). Fasten off.

Forget-Me-Not

This very quick and easy little flower in two colours can be used in the same way as the Buttercup or even sprinkled among buttercups in a project.

With yellow, ch2 making sure the slip knot will tighten from the tail end.
Round 1 (RS): 5 dc in 2nd ch from hook, sl st in top of ch2 to join.
Change to blue.
Round 2: Ch3, 3tr in same st, ch3, sl st in same st, (sl st, ch3, 3tr, ch3, sl st) in each dc around, sl st in base of first ch3 to join (5 petals). Fasten off.

Daisy

The centre can be made a little smaller than the one shown, but there will be fewer petals. Two stitches are required for each petal. Ideally select a bright colour for the centre and work the petals in a paler one. I used a warm yellow for the centre and white for the petals.

CENTRE

With yellow, ch2 ensuring the tail end tightens.
Round 1 (RS): 5 dc in 2nd ch from hook, sl st in top of ch2 to join (6 dc).
Round 2: Ch1 (counts as first dc), 1 dc in same place, 2 dc in each dc around, sl st in first ch to join (12 dc).
Round 3: Ch1 (counts as first dc), *2 dc in next dc, 1 dc in next dc; rep from * 4 times, 2 dc in next dc, sl st in first ch to join (18 dc). Fasten off leaving a long end for sewing.

PETALS

Hold the centre with RS facing; join white to any dc.
*Ch8, dc in 2nd ch from hook, 1 htr in next ch, 1 tr in next ch, 2 dtr in next ch, 1 tr in next ch, 1 htr in next ch, 1 dc in next ch, skip next dc on centre, sl st in next st, rep from * 8 times, sl st to base of first 8 ch. Fasten off white.
To complete, thread the yellow end into a tapestry needle and work the thread in and out of all the stitches on round 3 of the centre. Pull this tight to form a dome. The centre can be filled with a bead or some of the yellow yarn if desired, but this will depend on what the flower is to be used for.

Wild Rose

This flower can be made in one colour or in three colours as pictured. It can also look attractive if either the Buttercup or the Forget-Me-Not is placed in its centre. I used pale green for the centre, pink for the centre part of the petal and lilac to edge the petals.

With pale green ch5, join into a ring with sl st in first ch.
Round 1: Ch1 (counts as first dc), 9 dc in ring, sl st in first ch to join (10 dc).
Round 2: *Ch4, skip next dc, 1 dc in next dc; rep from * 4 times, sl st in base of first 4 ch (5 loops). Fasten off green; join pink.
Round 3: Work (1 dc, ch3, 1 dtr, 3 trtr, 3 quadtr, 3 trtr, 1 dtr, ch3, 1 dc) in each ch-4 sp around, sl st in first dc to join (5 petals). Fasten off pink; join lilac.
Round 4: *1 dc into each of next 3 ch, 1dc in next tr, 2 tr in each of next 3 sts, (1 tr, 1 dc) in next st, 2 dc in next st, (1 dc, 1 tr) in next st, 2 tr in each of next 3 sts, 1 dc in next st, 1 dc in each of next 3 ch; rep from * around, sl st in first sc to join. Fasten off.

Patterns

Now we have explored the techniques it's
time to put them to use and reap the rewards.
From a stylish evening top to an outdoor
jumper to an Aran cardigan, these projects are
designed to inspire and incorporate many of
the techniques found throughout the book.

7

Evening Warmth

Evening Warmth is a cleverly designed style for those special events when you do not want to spoil your makeup or your hairdo. Fastening on the shoulder and at the side, the design allows this tabard-style vest to wrap around your outfit. A luxury yarn requires only a simple stitch. Minimal embellishment ensures the garment can be worn for many different festivities. Make a variety of flower motifs in diverse colours in advance (each backed with a brooch pin). Choose the one that goes best with the outfit.

SKILL
Easy

SIZE
Directions are given for size Medium. Changes for Large and Extra Large are in parentheses.

FINISHED BUST
96.5(112:127)cm (38[44:50]in). To fit up to a 91.5cm (36in) (Medium), 106.5cm (42in) (Large) and 122cm (48in) (Extra Large) bust.

FINISHED LENGTH
63.5cm (25in) all sizes.

MATERIALS
• Rowan Natural Silk Aran, 73% viscose/15% silk/12% linen, (65m [71yd] per 50g [1.75oz] ball): 10(11:13) balls #465 black.
• Optional for the two border rows: 28g [1oz] Lucci Sequin yarn or sequins threaded onto a reel of invisible sewing thread. This is worked together with the yarn.
• 7.00mm (K-10.5) crochet hook or size needed to obtain tension.
• 6 buttons (2.8cm [1⅛in]).

TENSION
8 sts and 6 rows in tr = 10cm (4in).

TO MAKE
Back and Front are worked in one piece starting with back, working over one shoulder, then working front.

BACK
Ch41(47,53).
Row 1: 2 tr in 5th ch from hook, *skip 1 ch, 2 tr in next ch (V-st made), rep from * to last 2 ch, 1 tr in last ch. (38[44:50] sts)
Row 2: Ch3 (counts as tr), skip first 2 tr, *2 tr between 2 tr of V-st (V-st made), rep from * to last tr, skip next tr, 1 tr in top of turning ch, turn. (18[21:24] V-sts)
Repeat row 2 (40 times) more for all sizes or until work measures 63.5cm (25in) from beginning.

FRONT
Divide for Neck
Ch3 (counts as tr), work V-st in each of next 5(6:7) V-sts, 1 tr in first tr of next V-st, ch29(33:37) for neck and left shoulder.
Next row: 2 tr in 5th ch from hook, *skip next ch, 2 tr in next ch (V-st made), rep from * 13(15:17) times across added ch, 1 tr in next tr, work V-st in each of next 6(8:10) V-sts, 1 tr in top of 3 ch. Repeat row 2 (39 times). Fasten off.

Preparation for Border
Secure all ends.
Starting 25.5cm (10in) below the shoulder seam on right side, join the side seam for 15cm (6in), making sure the bottom two corners are level and the number of rows from the two corners to the end of the join are equal. Leave the other side open.
The opening should be on the left-hand side of the garment. Exactly opposite the join on the open side at the front of the work, mark the position for three buttons, evenly spaced.
Mark the position for three buttons evenly across the front opening of the

shoulder using 6(8:10) V-sts counting from the open corner.

Armhole Border

Round 1: Join the yarn together with the Sequin yarn to the armhole edge of the side seam, ch1, dc evenly around armhole, join with sl st in first dc, do not turn work.

Round 2: Working from left to right, crab st in each dc around, join with sl st in first crab st. Fasten off.

Garment Border

Round 1: With right side facing, join the yarn together with the Sequin yarn to the centre back neck, 1 dc in each st to corner, 2 dc in corner st, dc down open side of back, 2 dc in corner st, dc evenly across bottom edge of back, 2 dc in corner st, dc up back to seam closure, dc down front for vent, 2 dc in corner st, dc evenly across bottom edge of front, 2 dc in corner st, (dc up front to button marker, ch5, 1 dc in next st) 3 times, dc up front to corner, 2 dc in corner st, dc to last st across front neck, dc2tog using 1 st from front neck and 1 st from shoulder, 1 dc in shoulder, dc2tog using 1 st from shoulder and 1 st from back neck, dc to start of round, join with sl st in first dc. Do not turn work.

Round 2: Working from left to right, (crab st in each dc to ch-5 loop, 6 dc in ch-5 loop) 3 times (there is no need to put an extra st in the corners), crab st in each st to beginning of round, join with sl st in first crab st. Fasten off.

FINISHING

Sew the buttons to the back opposite button loops worked on the front. Embellish with a motif or flower.

For schematic, see page 108

Hug-Me-Tight Vest

Hug-Me-Tight Vest is neat and crisp. The counterpane stitch, simple borders, and covered buttons are ideal for this classic design.

SKILL
Easy

SIZE
Directions are given for size Small. Changes for Medium, Large, and Extra Large are in parentheses.

FINISHED BUST
91.5 (106.5:117:127)cm (36[42:46:50]in). To fit up to a 86.5cm (34in) (Small), 96.5cm (38in) (Medium), 106.5cm (42in) (Large) and 122cm (48in) (Extra Large) bust.

FINISHED LENGTH
45.5cm (18in) all sizes.

MATERIALS
• Rowan Cashsoft DK, 57% extra-fine merino wool/33% microfibre/10% cashmere, (130m [142yd] per 50g [1.75oz] ball): 7(8:9:9) balls #501 sweet.
• 4.00mm (G-6) crochet hook or size needed to obtain tension.
• 4 buttons to fill button casings (1.6cm [⅝in]).

TENSION
16 sts and 14 rows in pattern = 10cm (4in).

TO MAKE
Back and Front are worked in one piece starting with back, working over each shoulder, then working fronts separately.
Chain 74(84:92:102).
Row 1 (right side): 1 dc in 3rd ch from hook, 1 dc in each remaining ch.
Row 2: Ch3 (counts as first tr), *1 dc in next st, 1 tr in next st, rep from * to end. (73[83:91:101] sts)
Row 3: Ch1 (counts as first dc), *1 tr in next dc, 1 dc in next tr, rep from * to end.
Repeat rows 2 and 3 until work measures 40.5cm (16in) from beginning, ending with row 3.
Divide for fronts.

RIGHT FRONT
Next row: 3 ch (counts as tr), *1 dc in next tr, 1 tr in next dc, rep from * 11(14:16:18) times, turn, leaving remaining sts unworked.
(25[31:35:39] sts)
Next row: Repeat row 3 on these 25(31:35:39) sts.
Work rows 2 and 3 until front measures 16.5cm (6½in) from shoulder, ending with row 3.
Next row (increase row): Ch3 (counts as tr), *1 dc in next tr, 1 tr in next dc, rep from * to end, ending with (tr, dc) in last st, turn.
Next row: Ch3 (counts as tr), 1 dc in next tr, *1 tr in next dc, 1 dc in next tr, rep from * to end.
Maintaining established pattern, increase 1 st at neck edge every other row until 41(46:50:55) sts are on work. Then work even in pattern until front measures 40.5cm (16in) from beginning. Fasten off.

LEFT FRONT
Next row: With right side facing, skip next 23(21:21:23) sts to the left of last st made in first row of right front, join yarn in next st, 3 ch (counts as tr), *1 dc

in next tr, 1 tr in next dc, rep from *
11(14:16:18) times, turn. (25[31:35:39]
sts)

Next row: Repeat row 3 on these
25(31:35:39) sts.
Works rows 2 and 3 until front
measures 16.5cm (6½in) from shoulder,
ending with row 3.

Next row (increase row): Ch1 (counts as
first dc), 1 tr in first st, *1 dc in next tr,
1 tr in next dc, rep from * to end.

Next row: Ch1 (counts as first dc), *1 tr
in next dc, 1 dc in next tr, rep from * to
end, ending with tr in top of turning
ch, turn.
Maintaining established pattern,
increase 1 st at neck edge every other
row until 41(46:50:55) sts are on work.
Then work even in pattern until front
measures 40.5cm (16in) from beginning.
Fasten off.
Fold the two fronts to lie on the back
with right sides facing. Leaving 23cm
(9in) open for armholes, sew fronts
to back across bottom 18cm (7in) on
each side.

ARMHOLE BORDERS

Round 1: With right side facing, join
yarn at bottom of one armhole, ch1, dc
evenly around, join with sl st in first dc.
Round 2: Ch1, working from left to
right, crab st in each dc around, join
with sl st in first crab st. Fasten off.

FRONT AND NECK BAND

Row 1: With right side facing, join yarn
at bottom of right front edge, ch1, dc
evenly up right front, across back neck
edge, down left front edge to bottom
left-hand corner, do not turn.
Row 2: Ch1, working from left to right,
crab st in each dc to end. Fasten off.

WAISTBAND

Row 1: With right side facing, join yarn
to bottom edge at left front corner,
1 ch, dc evenly bottom edge to right
front corner, turn.

Rows 2–3: Ch1, dc in each dc to end,
turn.
Mark the positions for two buttonholes
approximately 3.8cm (1½in) apart on
right front. (See photo for position
guidance.)
Row 4 (buttonhole row): Ch1, *1 dc in
each dc to next marker, ch2, skip 2 dc,
rep from * once, dc in each dc to end,
turn.
Row 5: Ch1, *1 dc in each dc to next ch-2
sp, 2 dc in in next ch-2 sp, rep from *
once, dc in each dc to end, turn.
Rows 6–8: Ch1, dc in each dc to end,
turn.
Rows 9–13: Rep rows 4–8. Fasten off.

BOTTOM EDGING

Row 1: With right side facing, join yarn
to the last crab st on the right front
edge, ch1, crab st evenly across side
edge of waistband, across entire
bottom edge, then up left edge of
waistband, sl st in the first crab st of
the front and neck band. Fasten off.
Work four button casings, inserting
buttons for firmness. Attach to the
waistband.

For schematic, see page 108

Cosy Jumper

Cosy Jumper incorporates the interesting technique of turning on every other row. It has side pockets, a high neck, long sleeves and is worked in pure wool – making it ideal outdoor wear whatever the season.

SKILL
Intermediate

SIZE
Directions are given for size Small. Changes for Medium, Large, and Extra Large are in parentheses.

FINISHED BUST
96.5(106.5:119.5:129.5)cm (38[42:47:51]in). To fit up to a 86.5cm (34in) (Small), 96.5cm (38in) (Medium), 106.5cm (42in) (Large) and 117cm (46in) (Extra Large) bust.

FINISHED LENGTH
53.5cm (21in) all sizes.

MATERIALS
• Rowan Scottish Tweed 4-ply, 100% wool, 131m ([120yd] per 25g [⅞oz] ball): 10(12:14:16) balls #0013 Claret (main colour: MC) and 3(4:4:5) balls in #0024 Porridge (contrast colour: CC).
• 4.00mm (G-6) and 5.00mm (H-8) crochet hooks or sizes needed to obtain tension.

TENSION
With 4.00mm (G-6) hook 18 sts and 13 rows = 10cm (4in) in pattern stitch.

PATTERN STITCH
Turn the work on every other row when both colours are at the same end.
Row 1: With MC, ch3 (counts as tr), 1 tr in each st to end, do not turn.
Row 2: With CC, ch2 (counts as htr), 1 htr in each st to end, turn.
Row 3: With MC, ch1 (counts as dc), 1 dc in each st to end, do not turn.
Row 4: With CC, ch3 (counts as tr), 1 tr in each st to end, turn.
Row 5: With MC, ch2 (counts as htr), 1 htr in each st to end, do not turn.
Row 6: With CC, ch1 (counts as dc), 1 dc in each st to end, turn.

TO MAKE
Back and Front worked in one piece starting at a side edge.

FIRST SIDE
With 4.00mm (G-6) hook, ch193.
Row 1: Tr in 4th ch from hook, tr in each ch across, turn. (191 sts)
Starting with row 2, work in Pattern Stitch for 20(24:26:30) rows more.

CENTRE BACK
Continue working in Pattern Stitch on first 91 sts for next 19(19:21:21) rows. Keep the pattern continuous even if this requires breaking off one of the yarns and rejoining it at the other end of the row. After working for 19(19:21:21) rows, fasten off both yarns.

CENTRE FRONT
Skip 8 sts, rejoining the same yarn used for the first row of centre back in the next st, continue in Pattern Stitch to end of row (92 sts). Join in other yarn at the appropriate place. Decrease 1 st at the neck edge only on each of next 5 rows. Maintaining pattern, work 9(9:11:11) rows even. Increase 1 st at the neck edge only on each of next 5 rows.

SECOND SIDE
If the last row of front ends at the neck edge, work 8 ch, sl st in first st on last row of back. Fasten off.
If the last row of front ends at the hem edge, using matching colour, join yarn in last st of last row of back, ch 8, sl st in last st of last row of front. Fasten off. (191 sts) Continue in Pattern Stitch on 191 sts for 21(25:27:31) rows. Fasten off.

BOTTOM RIB
Row 1: With right side facing, using MC and 5.00mm (H-8) hook, join yarn at

lower right-hand corner of back, ch2, work 63(63:67:67) htr evenly spaced across the row ends of the back, turn. (64[64:68:68] htr)

Row 2: Ch2 (counts as first st), *FPtr around the post of next st, BPtr around the post of next st; rep from * across, ending with htr in corner st, turn.

Rows 3–7: Rep row 2. Fasten off. Rep bottom rib on bottom edge of front.

FIRST SLEEVE

Row 1: With right side facing, using 4.00mm (G-6) hook, skip first 59(59:57:57) sts on last row on side edge, join appropriate yarn in next st, continue in pattern for 13 rows on the centre 73(73:77:77) sts. Decrease 1 st at each end of next row and every other row until 44 rows have been completed. (41[41:45:45] sts) Continue working in pattern without decreases until work measures 40.5(40.5:42:42)cm (16[16:16½:16½]in) from beginning, ending with any row that uses MC (the same colour as that for the cuffs). Do not fasten off. Change to 5.00mm (H-8) hook.

CUFF

Work in post tr ribbing until cuff measures 5cm (2in) from beginning. Fasten off.

SECOND SLEEVE

Row 1: With right side facing, using 4.00mm (G-6) hook, skip first 59(59:57:57) sts on other side edge, join appropriate yarn in next st, working in reverse order of pattern stitch (1 row dc, 1 row htr, 1 row tr) to match the pattern in the body of the garment, work even in pattern for 13 rows on the centre 73(73:77:77) sts.

Maintaining second sleeve pattern, finish sleeve same as first sleeve and cuff. Fasten off.

POCKET

With MC and 4.00mm (G-6) hook, ch27.

Row 1: 1 htr in 3rd ch from hook, 1 htr in each ch to end, turn. (26 htr)

Row 2: Ch2 (counts as htr), 1 htr in each st to end, turn.

Rep row 2 until work measures 23cm (9in) from beginning. Fasten off.

NECK BORDER

Before assembling the pieces, work the post stitch border for the neck as follows:

Round 1: With 5.00mm (H-8) hook, join MC in centre st on back neck edge, ch2 (counts as htr), work htr evenly around the neck opening, making sure you have enough stitches for head to fit through neck opening, ending with an even number of stitches, sl st in top of beginning ch2 to join, turn.

Round 2: Ch2 (counts as first st), *FPtr around the post of next st, BPtr around the post of next st; rep from * across to within last st, FPtr around the post of last st, sl st in top of beginning ch2 to join, turn.

Round 3: Ch2 (counts as first st), *BPtr around the post of next st, FPtr around the post of next st; rep from * across to within last st, BPtr around the post of next st, sl st in top of beginning ch to join, turn.

Rounds 4–5: Rep rounds 2–3 once. Change to 4.00mm (G-6) hook.

Rounds 6–7: Rep rounds 2–3 once. Fasten off.

FINISHING

Fold the pocket in half and seam across both short edges and for part of the long side. Insert the pocket in a side seam of the sweater. With pocket facing down, pin in position making sure that the back and the front have an equal number of stitches above and below the opening. Sew the pocket in place across corresponding sts on front and back. Repeat with other pocket. Sew remainder of side seams.

For schematic, see page 108

Aran Cardigan

Aran Cardigan includes Aran-style crochet with shadow stitches, a concealed zip and a hood. The post stitch rib adds a further detail, making this short jacket snug and comforting.

SKILL
Intermediate

SIZE
Directions are given for size Medium. Changes for Large and Extra Large are in parentheses.

FINISHED BUST
91.5(106.5:122)cm (36[42:48]in). To fit up to a 91.5cm (36in) (Medium), 106.5cm (42in) (Large) and 122cm (48in) (Extra Large) bust.

FINISHED LENGTH
51cm (20in) all sizes.

MATERIALS
• Rowan Pure Wool Aran, 100% wool, (170m [186yd] per 100g [3.5oz] ball): 7(9:10) balls #670 Ivory.
• 5.00mm (H-8) and 6.00mm (J-10) crochet hooks or sizes needed to obtain tension.
• One 45.5cm (18in) open-ended zip.
• 2 buttons (2.2cm [⅞in]) in diameter.

TENSION
With 6.00mm (J-10) hook, 12 sts and 7 rows in tr = 10cm (4in).

CABLE STITCH PATTERN WITH SPECIAL ABBREVIATIONS
Row 1: 1 tr in next st leaving 2 loops on hook (first st of shadow st), skip next 2 sts, 1 FPquadtr around the post of next st leaving 2 loops on hook, yo, pull through all 3 loops on hook (shadow st completed), 1 FPquadtr around the post of each of next 2 sts, 1 FPquadtr around the post same st as first st of shadow st, 1 FPquadtr around the post of first of 2 skipped sts, 1 FPquadtr around the post of next skipped st leaving 2 loops on hook, skip next 3 sts holding post sts, 1 tr in next st leaving 2 loops on hook, yo, pull through all 3 loops (1 FC made).
Row 2: 1 BPdtr around the post of each of next 6 sts of the cable (1 BC made).

TO MAKE
Back and Front worked in one piece to the armholes.
With 6.00mm (J-10) hook, ch110(128:146).
Row 1 (wrong side): 1 tr in 4th ch from hook, 1 tr in each ch to end, turn. (108[126:144] sts)
Row 2 (right side): Ch3 (counts as tr), 1 tr in each of next 5(6:7) sts, 1 FPtr around the post of next tr, 1 tr in each of next 2 tr, work 1 FC, 1 tr in each of next 2 tr, 1 FPtr around the post of next tr, 1 tr in each of next 86(100:116) tr, 1 FPtr around the post of next tr, 1 tr in each of next 2 tr, work 1 FC, 1 tr in each of next 2 tr, 1 FPtr around the post of next tr, 1 tr in each of last 6(7:8) tr, turn.
Row 3: Ch3 (counts as tr), 1 tr in each of next 5(6:7) tr, 1 BPtr around the post of next st, 1 tr in each of next 2 tr, work 1 BC, 1 tr in each of next 2 tr, 1 BPtr around the post of next st, 1 tr in each of next 86(100:116) tr, 1 BPtr around the post of next st, 1 tr in each of next 2 tr, work 1 BC, 1 tr in each of next 2 tr, 1 BPtr around the post of next st, 1 tr in each of last 6(7:8) tr, turn.
Rep rows 2 and 3 seven times.

Divide for Armholes

Right Front

Row 1 (right side): Ch3 (counts as tr), tr in each of next 5(6:7) sts, 1 FPdtr around the post of next tr, 1 tr in each of next 2 tr, work 1 FC, 1 tr in each of next 2 tr, 1 FPdtr around the post of next tr, 1 tr in each of next 8(12:16) tr, turn. (26[31:36] sts)

Row 2: Ch3 (counts as tr), 1 tr in each of next 7(11:15) tr, 1 BPdtr around the post of next st, 1 tr in each of next 2 tr, work 1 BC, 1 tr in each of next 2 tr, 1 BPdtr around the post of next st, 1 tr in each of last 6(7:8) tr, turn.

Rep rows 1 and 2 six times, then rep row 1 once.

Shape Neck

Next row: Ch3 (counts as tr), 1 tr in each of next 7(11:15) tr, 1 BPdtr around the post of next st, 1 tr in each of next 3 tr, turn, leaving remaining sts unworked. (12[16:20] sts)

Next row: Ch3 (counts as tr), 1 tr in each of next 2 tr, 1 FPdtr around the post of next st, 1 tr in each of next 8(12:16) tr, turn.

Next row: Ch3 (counts as tr), 1 tr in each st to end, turn.

Next row: Rep last row. Fasten off.

BACK

Row 1: With right side facing, skip 4 sts to the left of last st made in first row of right front, join yarn to next st, ch3 (counts as tr), 1 tr in each of next 47(55:63) sts, turn, leaving remaining sts unworked. (48[56:64] sts)

Work even in tr for 14 rows. Fasten off.

LEFT FRONT

Row 1: With right side facing, skip 4 sts to the left of last st made in first row of back, join yarn to next st, ch3 (counts as tr), 1 tr in each of next 7(11:15) tr, 1 FPdtr around the post of next st, 1 tr in each of next 2 tr, work 1 FC, 1 tr in each of next 2 tr, 1 FPdtr around the post of next tr, 1 tr in each of next

6(7:8) tr, turn. (26[31:36] sts)

Row 2: Ch3 (counts as tr), 1 tr in each of next 5(6:7) tr, 1 BPdtr around the post of next st, 1 tr in each of next 2 tr, work 1 BC, 1 tr in each of next 2 tr, 1 BPdtr around the post of next st, 1 tr in each of next 8(12:16) tr, turn.

Rep rows 1 and 2 six times then rep row 1 once.

Shape Neck

Next row: Ch3 (counts as tr), 1 tr in each of next 2 tr, 1 BPdtr around the post of next st, 1 tr in each of next 8(12:16) tr, turn, leaving remaining sts unworked. (12[16:20] sts)

Next row: Ch3 (counts as tr), 1 tr in each of next 7(11:15) tr, 1 FPdtr around the post of next st, 1 tr in each of next 3 tr, turn.

Next row: Ch3 (counts as tr), 1 tr in each st across, turn. (12 sts)

Next row: Rep last row. Fasten off. Sew fronts to back at shoulders.

BOTTOM RIB

Row 1: With 5.00mm (H-8) hook and right side facing, join on bottom left-hand corner of left front, ch2, *FPtr around the post of next st, BPtr around the post of next st; rep from * across entire bottom edge to right front corner, htr in corner st, turn.

Rows 2–3: Rep row 1. Fasten off.

SLEEVES (MAKE 2)

(All sizes)

With 6.00mm (J-10) hook, loosely ch58. It is important that the chain is loose or it will not fit into the armhole easily.

Row 1: 1 tr in 4th ch from hook, 1 tr in each ch to end, turn. (56 sts)

Row 2: Ch3 (counts as tr), 1 tr in each tr to end, turn.

Rows 3–4: Rep row 2.

Tip: Check whether the sleeve will fit into the armhole opening at this point.

Row 5: Ch3 (counts as tr), tr2tog in next 2 sts, tr in each tr to end, turn. (1 dec made)

For schematic, see page 109

Work in tr, decreasing 1 st at the beginning of each row until 32 sts remain. Work even in tr until sleeve measures 44.5cm (17½in) from beginning or desired length.

CUFF

Row 1: Change to 5.00mm (H-8) hook, ch2, *1 FPtr around the post of next st, 1 BPtr around the post of next st; rep from * to end, 1 htr in corner st, turn.
Rows 2–3: Rep row 1. Fasten off.

RIGHT FRONT BANDS (TO BE WORKED BEFORE THE HOOD)

Row 1: With 5.00mm (H-8) hook and right side facing, join yarn at bottom right-hand corner of right front edge, ch1, 1 dc in same place, *1 dc in next row-end st, 2 dc in next row-end st, rep from * across to top right-hand corner of right front, 1 dc in last st, do not turn.
Row 2: Ch1, working from left to right, crab st in each dc across. Fasten off.

LEFT FRONT BAND

With 5.00mm (H-8) hook and right side facing, join yarn at top right-hand corner of left front edge, rep rows 1 and 2 of right front band. Fasten off.

HOOD

Row 1: With 5.00mm (H-8) hook, join yarn first st on neck edge of right front, ch1, tr in each of next 5(6:7) sts, (tr2tog in next 2 sts) 3 times, tr3tog using 2 sts on front and 1 st on side, tr evenly across shoulder, tr3tog using 1 st on side and 2 sts on back, *1 tr in each of next 2 tr, tr2tog in next 2 sts, rep from * across back to within last 2 sts, tr3tog using 2 sts on back and 1 st on side, tr evenly across shoulder, tr3tog using 1 st on side and 2 sts on front, (tr2tog in next 2 sts) 3 times, 1 tr in each tr across to left front corner st, turn.
Work even in tr on these sts until work measures 33cm (13in) from beginning. Fasten off.

HOOD BORDER

Row 1: With right side facing, join yarn in left-hand corner of hood, ch1, dc evenly across front edge of hood, do not turn.
Row 2: Ch1, working from left to right, crab st in each sc across. Fasten off.

BUTTON TAB

With 5.00mm (H-8) hook, ch6.
Row 1: 1 dc in 3rd ch from hook, 1 dc in each ch to end, turn. (5 sts)
Row 2: Ch1 (counts as dc), 1 dc in each st to end, 1 dc in top of turning ch, turn.
Row 3 (buttonhole row): Ch1, 1 dc in next dc, ch1, skip next dc, 1 dc in each of next 2 sts, turn.

Row 4: Ch1, 1 dc in next st, 1 dc in next ch-1 sp, 1 dc in each of next 2 sts, turn.
Rows 5–7: Rep row 2.
Rows 8–9: Rep rows 3 and 4.
Row 10: Rep row 2. Fasten off.

FINISHING

Sew sleeve seams. Inset sleeves in armholes and sew in place. With sewing needle and thread, sew zip to front edges. Sew one button on either side of hood approximately 5cm (2in) above neck edge. Button with button tab. Weave in all ends.

Peppermint Dress

Peppermint Dress is flattering and feminine, made of a soft yarn in a stitch pattern that hints at lace. A mercerised thread is used to frame each piece.

SKILL
Experienced

SIZE
Directions are given for size Medium. Changes for Large are in parentheses.

FINISHED BUST
96.5(106.5)cm (38[42]in). To fit up to a 91.5cm (36in) (Medium) and 101.5cm (40in) (Large) bust.

FINISHED SKIRT LENGTH
63.5cm (25in) for all sizes.

MATERIALS
• Rowan Cashcotton 4-ply, 35% cotton/25% polyamide/ 18% angora/13% viscose/ 9% cashmere, (180m [197yd] per 50g [1.75oz] ball): 10(11) balls #913 Peppermint (A).
• Number 10 crochet cotton in a complementary colour, 100% cotton, (266m [290yd] per 50g [1.75oz] ball): 2(2)balls in Light Green (B).
• 4.50mm (G-6) and 2.00mm (B-1) crochet hooks or size needed to obtain tension.
• 7 buttons 1.1cm (⁷/₁₆ in) in diameter.

TENSION
With A and 4.50mm (G-6) hook, 20 sts and 12 rows in back pattern = 10cm (4in).

TO MAKE

BACK
With A and 4.50mm (G-6) hook, ch70(80).
Row 1: 1 htr in 3rd ch from hook, *ch1, skip next ch, 1 htr in next ch, rep from * to end, turn. (69[79] sts)

Row 2: Ch3 (counts as htr, ch1), *1 htr in next ch-1 sp, ch1, rep from * to last 2 sts, skip next htr, 1 htr in top of turning ch, turn.
Row 3: Ch2 (counts as htr), *1 htr in next ch-1 sp, ch1, rep from * to last 2 sts, 1 htr in next ch-1 sp, 1 htr in top of turning ch.
Row 4: Rep row 2.
Row 5: Ch3 (counts as htr, ch1) (inc made), *1 htr in next ch-1 sp, ch1, rep from * to last st, 1 htr in top of turning ch (inc made), turn. (73[83] sts)
Row 6: Rep row 3.
Row 7: Ch2 (counts as htr), 1 htr in first st (inc made), *1 htr in next ch-1 sp, ch1, rep from * to last 2 sts, 2 htr in top of turning ch (inc made), turn. (75[85] sts)
Rows 8–21: Continue increasing on every other row by repeating rows 4–7 until there are 89(99) sts.
Rep rows 2 and 3 until work measures 23cm (9in) from beginning, ending with row 2 of pattern.

Shape Armhole
Armhole row: Sl st over first 10 sts, ch2 (counts as htr), *1 htr in next ch-1 sp, ch1, rep from across to last 11 sts, 1 htr in next st, turn, leaving last 10 sts unworked.
Rep rows 2 and 3 until work measures 25.5cm (10in) from beginning of armhole. Fasten off.

BORDER FRAME FOR BACK
Border rnd 1: With right side facing, using 2.00mm (B-1) hook, join yarn B in top left-hand corner of right armhole, ch1, dc evenly around back, working 3 dc over 2 row-end stitches up the armhole edge, working 2 dc at each corner, and working 2 dc in each st across top and bottom edge (working 1 dc in the front loop and 1 dc in the back loop), and working dc3tog at each inner corner at underarms, sl st in first dc to join.
Border rnd 2: Ch3 (count as tr), *skip

next 2 sts, (1 tr, ch2, 1 tr) in next dc, rep from * all round the back piece adapting pattern at corners, ending with (tr, ch2) in first dc, sl st in 3rd ch of beginning ch to join.

FRONT

Work same as back through first row of armhole.
Rep rows 2 and 3 three times.
Divide for neck.

FIRST SIDE

Neck row 1: Ch3 (counts as htr, ch1), *1 htr in next ch-1 sp, ch1, rep from * 13(15) times, 1 htr in next ch-1 sp, turn, leaving remaining sts unworked. (31[35] sts)
Neck row 2: Ch2 (counts as htr), *1 htr in next ch-1 sp, ch1, rep from * to last ch-1 sp, 1 htr in next ch-1 sp, 1 htr in 2nd ch of turning ch, turn.
Neck row 3 (dec row): Ch3 (counts as htr, ch1), *1 htr in next ch-1 sp, ch1, rep from * to end, omitting last ch, 1 htr in top of turning ch (dec made), turn. (30 [34] sts)
Neck row 4: Ch3 (counts as htr, ch1), *1 htr in next ch-1 sp, ch1, rep from * to last ch-1 sp, 1 htr in next ch-1 sp, 1 htr in 2nd ch of turning ch, turn.
Neck row 5 (dec row): Ch3 (counts as htr, ch1), *1 htr in next ch-1 sp, ch1, rep from * to last 3 sts, skip next (htr, ch1), 1 htr in 2nd ch of turning ch (dec made), turn. (29 [33] sts)
Neck row 6: Ch2 (counts as htr), *1 htr in next ch-1 sp, ch1, rep from * to last ch-1 sp, 1 htr in next ch-1 sp, 1 htr in 2nd ch of turning ch, turn.
Neck row 7: Rep row 3.
Continue in pattern, decreasing 1 st at neck edge on every other row in this manner until 23(27) sts remain. Work even in pattern until the front armhole measures the same as the back armhole.

SECOND SIDE

Skip 7(9) sts to the left of last st made in neck row 1 on first side, using 4.50mm (G-6) hook, join yarn A in next htr.
Neck row 1: Ch3 (counts as htr, ch1), *1 htr in next ch-1 sp, ch1, rep from * 13(15) times, 1 htr in top of turning ch, turn.
Neck row 2: Ch2 (counts as htr), *1 htr in next ch-1 sp, ch1, rep from * to last ch-1 sp, 1 htr in next ch-1 sp, 1 htr in 2nd ch of turning ch, turn.
Continue in pattern, decreasing 1 st at the neck edge on next row and every other row thereafter until 23(27) sts remain. Work even in pattern until armhole measures same as first side.

BORDER FRAME FOR FRONT

Rep back border around front, taking extra care to work pattern neatly on rnd 2 where the work divides for the neck.
Using a faggot join as described on page 42, connect the front shoulders to the back.

SLEEVE (MAKE 2)

Both sizes are worked the same.
With 4.50mm (G-6) hook and yarn A, ch80.
Row 1: 1 htr in 3rd ch from hook, *ch1, skip next ch, 1 htr in next ch, rep from * to last ch, htr in last ch, turn. (79 sts)
Row 2: Ch3 (counts as htr, ch1), *1 htr in next ch-1 sp, 1 ch, rep from * to last st, 1 htr in top of turning ch.
Row 3: Ch2 (counts as htr), *1 htr in next ch-1 sp, 1 ch, rep from * to last ch-1 sp, 1 htr in next ch-1 sp, 1 htr in 2nd ch of turning ch, turn.
Rows 4–6: Rep rows 2 and 3 once, then rep row 2 once more.

SLEEVE BORDER

Border rnd 1: With right side facing, using 2.00mm (B-1) hook, join yarn B in last st of last row of sleeve, ch1, dc evenly around sleeve, working 3 dc over 2 row-end stitches up the short edges, working 2 dc at each corner, and working 2 dc in each st across top and bottom edges, working 1 dc in the front loop and 1 dc in the back loop, sl st in first sc to join.
Border rnd 2: Ch3 (count as tr), *skip next 2 sts, (1 tr, ch2, 1 tr) in next dc, rep from * all round the sleeve adapting pattern at corners, ending with (tr, ch2) in first dc, sl st in 3rd ch of beginning ch to join.
Border edge: Working across long edge of sleeve, ch3, *tr2tog placing first st in next tr and second st in next tr skipping 2 ch between, ch4, 1 dc in 3rd ch from hook (1 picot made), ch1, rep from * across long edge of sleeve, 1 dc in last st. Do not put this border down the sides or along the base of the sleeve. Using a faggot join, insert the sleeves into the armholes.

NECK BORDER

Border edge: With right side facing, using 2.00mm (B-1) hook, join yarn B in left shoulder seam on neck edge, ch3, *tr2tog worked across next 2 tr, skipping ch2 between, ch1, picot, ch1, rep from * around, ending with sl st in 3rd ch of beginning ch to join.
Work the border edge around the neck, again taking care the picots are evenly spaced, particularly at the centre front.
Using a faggot join, connect the right-hand side of the bodice together.
Using a faggot join, connect the left-hand side of the bodice together leaving bottom 6.5cm (2½in) open.

SKIRT PANEL (MAKE 6)

With 4.50mm (G-6) hook and soft cotton make ch22(26).
Row 1: 1 htr in 3rd ch from hook, *ch1, skip 1 ch, 1 htr in next ch, rep from * across to within last ch, 1 htr in last ch, turn.
Row 2: Ch3 (counts as htr, ch1), *1 htr in next ch-1 sp, 1 ch, rep from * across

to last st, 1 htr in top of turning ch. (21[25] sts)

Row 3: Ch3 (counts as htr, ch1) (inc made), *1 htr in next ch-1 sp, ch1, rep from * to last st, 1 htr in top of turning ch (inc made), turn. (23[27] sts)

Row 4: Ch2 (counts as htr), *1 htr in next ch-1 sp, 1 ch, rep from * to turning ch, 1 htr in 2nd ch of turning ch, turn.

Row 5: Ch2 (counts as htr), 1 htr in first st (inc made), *1 htr in next ch-1 sp, ch1, rep from * to last 2 sts, 2 htr in top of turning ch (inc made), turn. (25[29] sts)

Row 6: Ch3 (counts as htr, ch1), *1 htr in next ch-1 sp, 1 ch, rep from * to last st, 1 htr in top of turning ch, turn.

Row 7: Ch2 (counts as htr), *1 htr in next ch-1 sp, 1 ch, rep from * to last ch-1 sp, 1 htr in last ch-1 sp, 1 htr in 2nd ch of turning ch, turn.

Row 8: Ch3 (counts as htr, ch1), *1 htr in next ch-1 sp, 1 ch, rep from * to last st, 1 htr in top of turning ch, turn.

Row 9: Ch3 (counts as htr, ch1) (inc made), *1 htr in next ch-1 sp, 1 ch, rep from * across to turning ch, 1 htr in last ch-1 sp, ch1, 1 htr in 2nd ch of turning ch (inc made), turn.

Rows 5 and 9 are increase rows. Working in established pattern, using the appropriate row to increase on rows 13, 17, 21, 25, 29, 41 and 57, continue to work in pattern until panel measures 61cm (24in) or desired length. Fasten off yarn A.

FIRST PANEL BORDER

With right side facing, using 2.00mm (B-1) hook, join yarn B in last st of last row of panel, work same as rnds 1 and 2 of sleeve border.

SECOND PANEL

Work same as first panel but do not fasten off yarn B after rnd 2 of border. Join this panel to the first panel with a faggot join described on page 42. Make and join 3 more panels.

Make the last panel in the same way and link the panel to the first panel made, leaving approximately 11.5cm (4½in) open at top of panels for the side opening.

BOTTOM BORDER

With right side facing, using 2.00mm (B-1) hook, join yarn B in any seam on bottom edge of skirt, ch3, *tr2tog worked across next 2 tr, skipping ch2 between, ch1, picot, ch1, rep from * around, ending with sl st in 3rd ch of beginning ch to join.

FINISHING

Pin the bodice to the skirt, matching the openings and ensuring the side opening of the bodice is aligned with the side opening of the skirt.

With right side facing, using 2.00mm (B-1) hook, join yarn B at top corner of skirt at side opening, working evenly around entire bodice and skirt, join the two pieces together with a faggot join, ending at other side of opening. Fasten off.

BACK OPENING BORDER

Row 1: With right side facing, using 2.00mm (B-1) hook, join yarn B to top of side opening on back, ch1, dc evenly across to bottom of opening, turn.

Row 2: Ch1, 1 dc in each dc across, turn.

Row 3: Rep row 2. Do not fasten off.

FRONT OPENING BORDER

Row 1: Dc evenly across front side of opening, turn.

Place seven markers, evenly spaced, across front edge for button loops.

Row 2: Ch1, *dc in each dc to next marker, ch6, sl st in same dc, 8 dc in ch-6 loop just made, rep from * to last marker, dc in each dc to end. Fasten off.

Sew buttons to back opening border opposite the button loops.

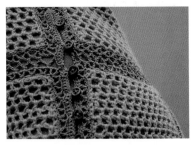

For schematic, see page 109

Schematics

Evening Warmth, see page 96

15(18:20)cm
(6[7:8]in)   18(20:23)cm
7[8:9]in)   15(18:20)cm
(6[7:8]in)

FRONT
AND
BACK

25cm
(10in)

15cm
(6in)

23cm
(9in)

48(56:64)cm
(19[22:25]in)

Hug-Me-Tight Vest, see page 98

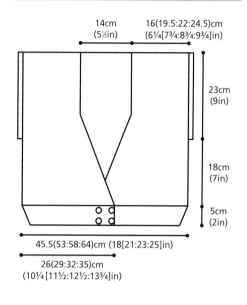

14cm
(5½in)   16(19.5:22:24.5)cm
(6¼[7¾:8¾:9¾]in)

23cm
(9in)

18cm
(7in)

5cm
(2in)

45.5(53:58:64)cm (18[21:23:25]in)

26(29:32:35)cm
(10¼[11½:12½:13¾]in)

Cosy Jumper, see page 100

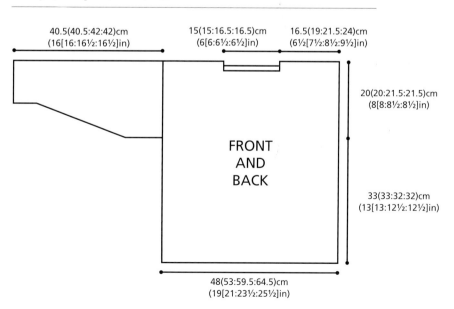

40.5(40.5:42:42)cm
(16[16:16½:16½]in)   15(15:16.5:16.5)cm
(6[6:6½:6½]in)   16.5(19:21.5:24)cm
(6½[7½:8½:9½]in)

FRONT
AND
BACK

20(20:21.5:21.5)cm
(8[8:8½:8½]in)

33(33:32:32)cm
(13[13:12½:12½]in)

48(53:59.5:64.5)cm
(19[21:23½:25½]in)

Aran Cardigan, see page 102

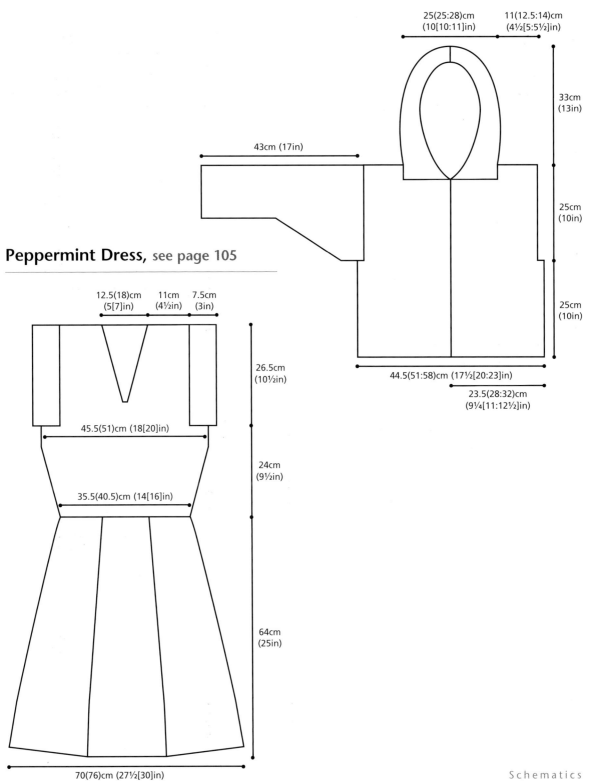

25(25:28)cm
(10[10:11]in)

11(12.5:14)cm
(4½[5:5½]in)

33cm
(13in)

43cm (17in)

25cm
(10in)

25cm
(10in)

44.5(51:58)cm (17½[20:23]in)

23.5(28:32)cm
(9¼[11:12½]in)

Peppermint Dress, see page 105

12.5(18)cm
(5[7]in)

11cm
(4½in)

7.5cm
(3in)

26.5cm
(10½in)

45.5(51)cm (18[20]in)

24cm
(9½in)

35.5(40.5)cm (14[16]in)

64cm
(25in)

70(76)cm (27½[30]in)

Abbreviations

approx	Approximately		inc	Increase
beg	Beginning		LS	Left side
BPtr	Back post stitch treble		m	Metres
ch	Chain		mm	Millimetres
ch sp	Chain Space		oz	Ounce
cm	Centimetres		patt	Pattern
cont	Continue		quadtr	Quadruple treble
dc	Double Crochet		rem	Remaining
dc2tog	Double Crochet two stitches together		rep	Repeat
			RS	Right side
dc3tog	Double Crochet three stitches together		tr2tog	Treble Crochet two stitches together
dec	Decrease		tr3tog	Treble Crochet three stitches together
dtr	Double Treble			
foll	Following		sk	Skip
FPquadtr	Front post stitch quadruple treble		sl st	Slip stitch
			sp	Space
FPtr	Front post stitch treble		st(s)	Stitch(es)
FPtrtr	Front post stitch triple treble		tch	Turning chain
			tog	Together
g	Gram		tr	Treble
htr	Half Treble Crochet		trtr	Triple treble
in	Inches		yo	Yarn over

Rowan yarns

UK

Rowan Yarns and Jaeger
Handknits
Green Lane Mill
Holmfirth, West Yorkshire
HD9 2DX
Tel: 01484 681881
www.knitrowan.com

USA

Westminster Fibers, Inc.
165 Ledge Street
Nashua, NH 03063
Tel: 1-800-445-9276
Website:
www.westminsterfibers.com
Email:
rowan@westminsterfibers.com

CANADA

Diamond Yarn
9697 St Laurent
Montreal, Quebec H3L 2N1
Tel: (514) 388 6188

Diamond Yarn (Toronto)
155 Martin Ross, Unit 3
Toronto, Ontario M3J 2L9
Tel: (416) 736 6111

AUSTRALIA

Rowan at Sunspun
185 Canterbury Road
Canterbury
Victoria 3126
Tel: 03 9830 1609

Index

Acknowledgements

I feel privileged to have been supported by wonderful people whilst writing this book:

My students from around the world who challenge and support me.

Katie Deane and the team at Collins & Brown who so professionally ensured the project succeeded.

Rowan yarns for providing the yarn.

Helen Jordan and Åsa who helped in the making of the projects.

Abby Franklin who designed these pages.

Caroline King for being my hands.

Picture credits:
Beauty photography by **Becky Maynes**
Step-by-step photography by **Michael Wicks**

Love crafts? Crafters… keep updated on all exciting craft news from Collins & Brown. Email **lovecrafts@anovabooks.com** to register for **free** email alerts on forthcoming titles and author events.